FREEDOM

A DIALOGUE

Ermanno Bencivenga

Translated from the Italian by the Author

Hackett Publishing Company, Inc.

Indianapolis/Cambridge

Copyright © 1997 by Hackett Publishing Company, Inc.

Printed in the United States of America

Text design by Dan Kirklin

02 01 00 99 98 97   1 2 3 4 5 6

For further information, please address

Hackett Publishing Company, Inc.
P.O. Box 44937
Indianapolis, Indiana 46244-0937

Library of Congress Cataloging-in-Publication Data

Bencivenga, Ermanno, 1950–
    [Libertà. English]
    Freedom: a dialogue/Ermanno Bencivenga; translated from the
Italian by the author.
       p.   cm.
    ISBN 0-87220-365-4 (cloth)   ISBN 0-87220-364-6 (pbk.)
    1. Philosophy. 2. Liberty. 3. Ethics. I. Title.
    B3613.B3835L5313 1997   97-24054
    196—dc21   CIP

To Enrico Forni and Corrado Mangione
who taught me much about life and freedom

FREEDOM

Preface

The publication in 1987 of *Kant's Copernican Revolution* represented for me the final outcome of years of research on the Kantian system. But, as often happens, this "representation" was to prove delusive: what I had understood as the conclusion of a phase of my work turned out to be only an initial step, the opening of a discourse. I had come to conceive Kant's fundamental contribution as a reorganization of logical space, as almost a gestalt switch, as the entering into a new world; so I felt a natural inclination to talk about that world, to try to describe the strange shapes I found there. Thus came *Tre dialoghi* (1988; translated as *Philosophy in Play* in 1994), *Looser Ends* (1989), and *The Discipline of Subjectivity* (1990), where themes of logic and epistemology, of aesthetics, metaphysics, and philosophy of language were discussed and analyzed from the point of view of the conceptual revolution Kant proposed. The present book (originally published in 1991) was one more stage in the same process, but a very important one for me because it signaled my return to the historical origins of that revolution. I have continued to speak about the world Kant showed to me, and about the ways he has taught me to think of my profession, but starting with this book I have also felt the need to speak once more about him. For many years now my courses and my studies have dealt extensively with Kant's moral philosophy, and with other moral philosophies that are necessary references for the Kantian position. In those courses and studies this book has been, for at least two years before its original publication, a precious tool: my research laboratory, the account of my wandering in that space where the "metaphysics of morals" originates. Only a few of the theses discussed in this book can be attributed directly to Kant, but the debate that takes place here provides the right context for locating the theses I intend to attribute to Kant, and for understanding how those theses can be developed or even (I say it with some trepidation, because with some people one *must* be modest) overcome. The main character in this book does not speak, and his position must be painstakingly reconstructed; it is important for me to emphasize that there is in the background another character who does not speak, and whom I am anxious to soon again call upon.

Roberto Casati and Paolo Leonardi discussed with me one of the many drafts of this book, and Paul Coppock has done precious editorial work on the first draft of my translation; I thank them for that. But my warmest thanks go to Nuccia Bencivenga, who read the whole manuscript in at least three of its incarnations, and gave me precious substantive and stylistic suggestions.

E.B.

Irvine, December 1996

One

STEFANO: But then is there any case in which you think it just to punish someone? If even in the face of a murder like this, so completely premeditated, so cold-blooded, you come up with your usual talk about society and the examples one received and education and subtle forms of conditioning and so on, where will you stop? How can you deny that Hitler too was unhappy as a child, that he too could not choose his conduct, that he too cannot be assigned any responsibility or guilt?

ROBERTO: I know you find my position irritating, Stefano, but for me it is never just to punish someone, since everyone—yes, even Hitler, it's better to be clear about it—everyone is determined by causal chains that make us find in something else, something he cannot be responsible for, the reasons for his action. And without responsibility, without freedom of choice, there can be no *just* praise or condemnation for any behavior: what "you did" has simply happened, and it's no more *yours* than a stone is when it hits you over the head as you walk by.

S: But that amounts to a reductio of all rules of human coexistence, all laws, all government!

R: Yes, within certain limits, but be careful about it. I am not denying that expressions like "it is just that" or "so and so is responsible for" are used, that a normative vocabulary has currency, nor do I think that such a vocabulary *ought not* to have currency: if I did, I would be involved in a curious pragmatic paradox. I am saying rather that I have no use for this vocabulary within my philosophical reconstruction of the world and of human experience. For me, as a philosopher, there are only facts in the world, and all facts can be explained, *that is*, reduced to other facts, deprived of their self-sufficiency, made dependent. Among the facts are the following: We commonly use normative expressions while repressing, penalizing, or promoting certain kinds of behavior. Such expressions are commonly included in attempts to justify that repression or promotion, and they have a basic role in intellectual structures intended to codify our notion of "socially acceptable." The explanation of *these* facts will be found in the history of a people or a group, and one will often establish that the adoption of certain values is functional to that people or group, at least in favoring its cohesiveness. All of this is very interesting, but does not force me to accept anything normative within my philosophical discourse. In that context, I need not ask whether a certain action is just, or free, or responsible; indeed I can deny the legitimacy of any such question as I study, with a naturalist's curiosity, the way in which it is phrased and addressed in a given community.

ENRICO: So yours is not so much a negative answer to Stefano's questions as a declaration that questions like that make no sense at all.

R: Exactly: it is a corrective answer, not a direct one. It rejects an implicit presupposition of those questions and invites us not to take them seriously. If you are asked, "When did you stop smoking?", you can answer, "Yesterday," or "Last year," but you can also answer, "I never smoked," or, "I never stopped," thus rejecting the question, indicating that there is something wrong with it, that it's generated by a wrong picture of things. Similarly, if you are asked, "When is it just to punish someone?", you can answer, "In such and such circumstances," or even "Never," but meaning by that—in the latter case—that after carefully examining all possible forms of punishment you have concluded that none is just. Answers like that accept the question, accept the research program it proposes, and present themselves as the result of executing that program. *My* answer, "Never," on the contrary, denies all sense to the inquiry itself, on the basis of an a priori argument that the use of normative terms is conceptually confused. Since all human behavior (including punishment and whatever is judged deserving of it) consists of events, and every event is a necessary consequence of other events, it is not legitimate to apply to any such behavior value judgments that presuppose a capacity to choose, a freedom which is entirely impossible.

E: But placing yourself outside the situation and refusing to use the same vocabulary as the subjects of your "study" will prevent you from entering into an effective relationship with them. You will only be able to observe them, to take notes as they massacre or exalt each other for ideal reasons which you will have to regard—all of them, indiscriminately—as delusive; you will be able to write down an accurate description of the facts but not, say, to encourage them to pursue a certain practice, or discourage them from another one, or influence them in any way. And this is a fairly depressing outcome when you consider that, despite your naturalist's attitude, you too belong to the zoo.

S: Yes, and in less fortunate circumstances you too would act without thinking about it much; you would not allow yourself the luxury of so many sophisms! Would you still be sitting around here involved in lovely conversation, debating freedom and determinism, if it were your daughter who had been tortured to death and buried in a cellar? Or wouldn't you rather be the first to demand justice, maybe even to take it in your own hands?

R: You're right, Stefano: I have been conditioned as much as anyone else. Therefore I too have irresistible "moral intuitions," and might express them by uttering appropriate judgments. I can say, "He's scum," or, "Human life is the most sacred thing," and I can even get myself in line to pull the trigger and "get rid of this monster" . . .

E: But, it seems, you can also emancipate yourself from such automatic reactions, float in the clear sky of rational reflection, and there capture the inevitable limitations of your unfortunate conspecifics.

R: "Emancipate" is a very delicate word, Enrico. I understand that it's in your interest to attribute it to me, so that you can later accuse me of contradicting myself. But I'd rather go about it more carefully, and just say that each of us is subject to different, even conflicting, sorts of conditioning, and that among those I received there is also one that opposes my "robust moral reactions" and lets me see my own and everyone else's morality with the detachment I was talking about.

S: A detachment you recommend, and hence one that belongs to your value system, to your morals. You too cannot do without norms.

R: We need to understand each other. If you take "true" to be a normative term then I too have my norms, but if you admit, as many do, that there is a difference between describing and *pre*scribing . . .

S: There are also many who question that difference.

R: If you insist, I will say that "true" is the only normative term I need. But notice how this term works. When things are seen with a naturalist's detachment then it's possible to see them as they *truly* are, but that's not to say that one ought to see them like that. At most it's to say that one ought to see them like that *if* one wants to see them as they are: a simple hypothetical imperative which does not require the adoption of any moral criterion or concept.

E: But I believe that the substance of my concern has not yet been addressed. That the *individual* Roberto, who is not only a philosopher but also a teacher, a father, a homeowner, and a citizen, can entertain moral sentiments and through them communicate and collaborate—or fight—with other people does not imply that the *philosopher* Roberto, and hence philosophy too, can ever establish such communication. Roberto will be able to survive in this world, a world of people, only to the extent that he's not, or no longer, a philosopher, and his philosophy will not help him: the facts it reveals to him will not tell him in which direction to go, what to do.

R: I disagree; I think, on the contrary, that often this rational activity will have extremely concrete results, with remarkable political and social significance. Take the case we started from. It is certainly dysfunctional for a society like ours to legalize murder, for such a practice would create serious instability and insecurity.

E: As in the Hobbesian state of nature?

R: Exactly. So we must find the best strategy to reduce the incidence of this kind of behavior, and there are various options. One could isolate real or even potential criminals; one could institute punishment as a deterrent; one could try to instill in all of us an irresistible horror of physical violence . . .

S: . . . maybe by making us see lots of movies.

R: To compare all these alternatives it will be necessary to carry out appropriate longitudinal studies, but in any case the problem is a factual one, and a solution must be found in terms of facts. It makes no sense to ask whether it's *just* to adopt certain measures, whether and to what extent there must be *retribution* for murderers, whether and to what extent a given individual is *guilty* for his actions—all confusing questions which are often a cover for oppressive practices or worse. How many of those who support the death penalty do so because they think that *one must* get an eye for an eye, or that persons of a certain kind, like this poor crazy guy . . .

S: Now you have blown *your* cover, now you have exposed the ideological underpinnings of your "rational" arguments! So the murderer is a "poor guy" now; it is him that we must pity! And his victims? Did *he* pity *them*?

R: OK, Stefano, to answer your provocations with one of mine, what would you say if one day a refrigerator started crushing people to death, or if an oven swallowed children and roasted them to perfection? You would pull their plugs, maybe you would destroy them, but certainly you would not think that they don't *deserve* to survive!

S: Don't change the subject now.

R: The subject is still the same. Did you ever hear people talk of "temporary insanity"? Some guy commits a murder and then it turns out that at the moment he did it—only at that moment, notice, not before or after—he had no understanding or will, and hence behaved with the same participation, the same capacity for free choice, as an oven or a refrigerator. What can you possibly do to someone like that? You can't punish him because he was not "responsible," it's not worth committing him to an institution because his insanity is an isolated and possibly unique episode . . .

S: Why? What would *you* do to him?

R: What to do to him is an empirical problem, to be faced with empirical tools. I don't have such tools and hence what I think about it is entirely irrelevant. Nor do I want to defend the use or the legitimacy of the concept of temporary insanity; on the contrary, it seems to me that the emergence of this concept within contemporary legal consciousness signals a basic embarrassment, a hesitation, a veiled recognition that the idea of justice as retribution is fundamentally wrong and confused, and that it must be totally abolished, together with all the intricate epicycles it's gotten us involved in.

E: So you are not interested in the murderer's mental state.

R: I am not interested in using it to determine his *guilt*. Trying to do so causes meaningless and dangerous judgments. If for example we proved that the death penalty is no deterrent, indeed that it might spur the elimination of inconvenient witnesses, and if we reached similar conclusions about incarceration and every other form of retribution practiced or practicable in our society, on what basis could we still justify the desire to return tit for tat?

E: So philosophy . . .

R: . . . clarifies the situation, lets us see beyond the "intuitions" and the invective that too often cloud our minds, and thus—even though it has nothing "practical" to suggest for the solution of concrete cases—

can have a strong (and, in my view, very useful) influence on the structure of our communal life.

E: Though it's understood that no one will ever be able to *decide* to act
in conformity with its conclusions.

R: Of course, if by "decide" we mean "freely decide." But this does
not entail that such conclusions, caused as they are (and as everything
else is) by other events through a necessary and unstoppable process,
cannot in turn originate just as necessarily a change in the environmen-
tal circumstances.

S: In short, are you opposed to convicting the defendant?

R: I am opposed to using words like "conviction" and "punishment,"
inherited from theological, irrational ages. We don't punish anyone for a
crime he's committed, but rather adopt measures which are more or less
functional for our survival and well-being as individuals and as a society.
This is what we *do*; then, with the sole result of muddying the waters
and troubling people's minds, we superimpose on it an idle "ethical" vocabulary, a pure and simple expression of our emotions and our confusion.

E: And if someone told you, on Freudian lines, that you are getting
things backwards: that it's not so much a matter of "superimposing" the
mystifying ideology of responsibility and guilt on already constituted
social practices, but rather of understanding society itself as the outcome of an original guilt?

R: Then I would say two things. First, Freud after all is on my side: the
guilt he talks about is an event, determined and "irresponsible" like any
other. It's guilt in a psychological, not a moral sense: guilt insofar as it is
felt as such. Second, the *use* of Freud you suggest (certain values have
preceded society historically, and made its constitution possible) represents the highest (or maybe the lowest) point of the ideology: when it
starts to invent "facts" (or better, "myths") in order to legitimize itself.

E: It sounds a little too simple to me. The relation between society
and guilt . . .

R: But why should truth be complicated? Sometimes I have the impression that you enjoy making your lives more difficult.

S: It's natural for you to have an "impression" like that, since you
don't realize how many implicit parameters there are in your discourse,
how many presuppositions *you* have. You translate normative terms into
apparently aseptic words like "useful" and "functional," and never for a
moment does it cross your mind to ask, "useful to whom?", "functional
for what purpose?" "The survival and well-being of individuals and so-

cieties," you say, but which individuals, which societies? What if it were a tyrant's survival, a gang's well-being? A few minutes ago you got away by citing hypothetical imperatives, but now this ploy comes back to haunt you. A hypothetical imperative does not stand on its own, by itself it doesn't tell you what to do, since it is indeed based on a hypothesis, and therefore implicitly raises the question of the desirability, the legitimacy, the morality of that hypothesis, and of its preferability to *other* hypotheses. But how can you answer such questions, given your a priori refusal of any categorical moral judgment, that is, of anything that might work as an ultimate premise for the chains of inconclusive conditionals you amuse yourself with in the course of your rational inquiry?

R: Take it easy; don't get too excited. If you scream so loud you will convince yourself that we disagree. But I subscribe to everything you said, or better, I subscribe to all the factual theses you uttered; then of course you are also implicitly suggesting that the position thus characterized is wrong, and here we have opposite views. But let's try to be clear about it. I am fully convinced that a rational inquiry cannot provide categorical premises of the kind you are looking for: it can only bring out conceptual connections and, through this process, can indeed rationalize our behavior, make it more effective for the realization of our goals. The goals, however, cannot come from the rational inquiry itself, and this is not a defect of such an inquiry but one of its features, just as it is not a defect but a feature of a hammer that one can only use it to hit something else, something different from the hammer. When I speak of survival as a goal I am only noticing that it *is* a goal for most organisms: individuals and societies, tyrants and saints, gangs and charities.

S: So you acknowledge that your position lacks an essential coordinate.

R: And that would be . . .

S: How to choose among these organisms, what survival to invest in.

R: But that's an essential coordinate for you, not for me! In fact, if I tried to insert it in my system somehow, I would end up contradicting myself, and then certainly what I say would be false. This way I can at least hope that it's true.

S: And as you strive so industriously for the truth, to what organisms will you bring your rationalizing contribution?

R: The only possible answer for me, you will realize, is: to the ones to which I am determined to bring it, that is (in general) the ones I identify with or belong to.

S: And don't you see the egocentrism of this position?

R: Yes, but I don't see why I should worry about it.

S: So for you it's perfectly fine to rationally pursue one's own survival and well-being and not give a damn about one's neighbor.

R: It's not *fine*; it simply *is*, it takes place, it happens, in most cases at least. Don't apply categories to my position that I consider meaningless. When it comes right down to it, your criticisms reduce to the fact that I don't take into account what matters to you.

BERTOLDO: This conclusion may be unfair, Roberto. Stefano has much more powerful weapons at his disposal, though so far he's chosen not to use them.

R: So use them yourself. Let's hear about them.

B: Through this whole discussion you have made a somewhat tendentious use of words like "fact" and "value" . . .

S: Not accidentally, considering his neopositivistic nonsense on the difference between *descriptive* and *prescriptive*.

B: . . . for example by hurriedly assigning to the realm of facts the universal statement that every event is necessitated by one or more causes. But, because this statement is indeed universal, no set of observed facts will ever be sufficient to verify it, and hence the statement will always remain a hypothesis, a bet. Some have even thought, as you know, that that's not even a statement but rather a rule of behavior: given an event, find its causes. Not a sentence in the indicative, therefore, but an imperative, a command, and a command is not too far from a value judgment.

R: I agree that someone *else* thought that. But I don't: as far as I am concerned, we really are talking about a statement, and it makes no difference that no one can ascertain its truth (or falsity) because it is something that *is* true or false anyway. Mountains have a height, so every mountain would have one even if there were mountains no one will ever be able to measure; thoughts on the other hand have no height, so it's inappropriate to ask about it. Less metaphorically, what you said does not have the least bit of relevance to the contrast I intend to set between facts and values: for me sentences like, "Murder is just (or unjust)," are not statements, they are neither true nor false, and that's not because we are not able to establish their truth or falsity, but because the notions of truth and falsity are entirely foreign to them.

B: OK; so let's take something whose truth can be established, for example the statement, "The pen in my pocket is red." How do you know that this statement is true, that it states a fact?

R: I compare it with my perception of the pen.

B: That is, you compare it with an experience, more precisely with a visual experience. In other circumstances you will attribute the same validating power to experiences of hearing, or touch, or smell.

R: Or taste, so we are done with all five senses.

B: With *those* five, yes: those of the empiricist tradition. But take now the statement, or if you prefer the sentence, "Murder is unjust." Can't you compare it with an experience that verifies it, exactly as you did with the pen? Don't you feel equally, or even more strongly, convinced that this sentence is correct?

R: Maybe, but it's a purely subjective conviction.

B: Why? Isn't it shared by most of humankind?

R: Yes, but everyone assents to it on his own, on the basis of his interior life, which cannot be compared with anyone else's. Only the end result coincides. The pen, however, is in a common space, accessible to everyone: *the same* pen, *the same* space.

B: Really? And how do you know that? How do you know that every one of us does not live in a private space of his own and does not relate to his own pen, his own phenomenal object? How do you know that it's not just the end result that coincides, in this case too?

R: If you want your hypothesis to be taken seriously, you must apply to it the same criteria of simplicity and economy every other hypothesis is subject to. And these criteria are not going to be very favorable to you; just think of the complications you would face in explaining how the various "phenomenal spaces" communicate with one another.

B: The alternative hypothesis might have problems that are just as serious, and maybe the same thing applies to our ethical judgments, but for the moment I want to limit myself to observing what follows: even if you were right that it's easier and more natural for us to explain visual perceptions in terms of a common space and moral experiences in terms of a private one, that might only mean that we are used to explaining them that way. What we are used to comes easier, but if it comes easier *because* we are used to it then certainly we cannot say that we have found a credible index of truth. Earlier you were talking of our ethical intuitions as the outcome of a conditioning process; but now it looks like a similar process might be at work in the realm of facts too, or better in the realm of those experiences we consider decisive in determining what is and what is not a fact.

E: Do you mean to say that there are no facts, or ultimate facts, or facts "in themselves"?

B: I'm not sure I *mean* to say anything. I have come to the conclusion that I am not one of those who have a message to communicate, a system to defend, a "categorical" judgment to impose. I am rather one who listens, and because I listen to this and that, I end up putting them together and seeing better the weaknesses of both—or the ways in which they might integrate each other. Here, specifically, I'm using lines I heard from Angelo . . .

E: That is, from someone whom, it seems, you have listened to a lot.

B: Yes, and yet I can't claim to be a faithful interpreter of his thought. There is a constant oscillation in him between two levels, between what he says and what he *does* by saying it, that is, the effect he produces by speaking of certain things in certain ways, between philosophy and rhetoric in short, and this odd, destabilizing methodology prevents one from attributing any position to him, even if he himself stated it.

E: Which incidentally would agree with the criticisms he brings against the notion of "the speaker's own" meaning, originating from his own *intention*.

B: You're right: it would agree with some of the things he says. But to which level do these things belong: to philosophy or rhetoric? Are they to be taken literally or do they rather have a secret "political" goal? I don't know, and maybe he doesn't know either, so all I can do is use in my own way, for my own purposes, sentences I heard him utter.

R: And what do these sentences say about facts? Do they deny them perhaps?

B: Not quite. They rather assert that the need for "facts" is a philosophical one, and hence one that has little to do with facts.

R: If this is a joke I don't find it funny. Try to make yourself clearer.

Two

BERTOLDO: I will try. Initially, Angelo has a position much like the one you were sketching earlier. Philosophy moves at a purely conceptual (he would say, "transcendental") level, and it's not concerned with establishing what happens or what there is in the world, but at most what it means to happen or to be in the world. Its area of maneuver is the logical space, not the real one: give it facts and it will ask about their meaning, it will compare them with a set of alternative possibilities, will attempt to uncover their structure. It will not be able to add or subtract anything from these facts: their factuality, their happening, is a pure and simple datum, an unquestionable starting point for its semantic articulation.

ROBERTO: So far so good.

B: I thought you would be happy so far, and so would many others. Despite the misunderstandings and the violent debates among philosophical schools, this general thesis would find almost everyone in agreement. With Angelo, however, the thesis occurs only initially. A philosophical discourse is an event that takes place in time, not an instant of eternity and coincidence: its logic involves diachrony and development, sometimes the negation of what has been, always at any rate a going elsewhere, a losing what was already said and an acquiring what must still be said.

ENRICO: You mean a dialectical process?

B: Maybe, but a dialectic purified of all the teleology and optimism of the Hegelian tradition, more or less stood on its head, and returned to the essential character of this movement, of this temporality which is *philosophy's* and not just its object's.

E: And is it through the movement you are talking about that Angelo goes from the transcendental/empirical distinction to the one between theory and practice, and then again the one between intellectuals and nonintellectuals, between the confabulating clowns locked in their ivory towers and the "one-dimensional" men carrying out their tasks with blind efficiency?

B: That's right, but there is another aspect of this movement—I would almost say, "another direction," except that everything feels connected in some obscure way, resonates with everything else—there is another more "speculative," less socio-political aspect which relates directly to the theme of our discussion. It's this: Take the man who acts at a practical level, who moves in a universe of facts and has not yet questioned their meaning or tried to dissect their logic . . .

STEFANO: Does such a man exist?

B: Maybe not, but if he doesn't that's not a problem. If anything, it further emphasizes the theoretical character of facts.

E: Let's try not to lose our thread.

B: OK. So one might say that our *homme machine* is not really involved in practices, that he does not really move in a factual context, because *he* does not have a point of view from which to perceive the practical and factual character of his behavior. It's *we* who, within a rational reconstruction of that behavior, for *our* purposes, create the reason/facts axis in order to situate and organize *our* interpretation of his world. It's we who, in particular, invoke that notion of theory for which practice becomes a necessary counterpart, which generates the need to refer to practice as an ineliminable parameter, and thus in the end *makes practice be* as something opposed to something else. For the wholly practical man, just because his acting is blind, automatic, and efficient, just because there is nothing other than that acting, just because theorizing is not part of his horizon, there arises no need to use a word like "practice."

R: Are you saying that for Angelo it would not be *true* to describe a man like that as involved in practical acting?

B: What he thinks of truth is a complex matter, and I'm not sure I understand too much of it. But we might be able to avoid such a thorny question: we might limit ourselves to saying that, in order to ask whether something is true, one must express that something, and our hypothetical one-dimensional man could not do it, could not describe himself as you suggested. Just as a certain historical figure became Cato Uticensis only after his death, only from the point of view on him that it then became possible to take, something becomes the universe of practices only when the practices are no longer the universe, the whole, only when there is something else with respect to which they can be practices.

R: You mean, "they can be *called* practices."

B: There is not much difference. Take this pen, and suppose there are two languages, L_1 and L_2. L_1 contains the word "pen," which refers to this kind of thing, inclusive of the cap; L_2, on the other hand, has no word "pen" but has the two words "pel," which refers to a pen without cap, and "pem," which refers to the cap. Suppose moreover that you speak L_2 but also have some rudimentary knowledge of L_1, and that someone asks you whether there is a pen here. You give him a strange look, think about it for a while, and then hazard: "Yes, there is one of those things that in L_1 are called pens."

R: I see where you are going: in the wake of "the sage of Königsberg," the world is not "given" independently of a conceptualization of it, and hence of a language expressing that conceptualization. But I don't find your example convincing, as I never do with these idealistic artifices, since in formulating it you (correctly) kept assuming that this was a pen and describing it as such. The fact that others might call it something else doesn't make it *be* something else: even if we called a dog's tail "leg," the dog would continue to have four legs.

B: I am not so sure: to express anything at all I must use a language, even to speak of another more or less fictitious language I must use my own, but it's dangerous to hypostatize one's own (meta)language so as to lose sight of the intrinsic relativity of every act of reference and judgment. If we called a dog's tail "leg" we would be speaking another language, and certainly in the original language the dog would continue to have four legs, but it would have five of them in the new language (or maybe only one, if there we called legs "tails").

E: Your views on this matter seem pretty clear, and clearly the consequence of opposite conceptions of the relation between language and reality. Shall we interrupt the digression and return to the main topic?

B: It was not a digression, Enrico: we never really left the "main" topic. We only embroidered it a bit, which helps one understand it better. But to summarize, since the "practical" man has no point of view from which it makes sense to speak of practices, to *call* something a practice, for him practices do not exist. In a world of practices alone—a world without theories—there are no practices. More generally: in a world of only facts—a purely empirical world, devoid of any conceptual dimension—there are no facts.

E: So facts are an invention of philosophers?

B: Let's rather say that they are a philosophical need, a condition of possibility for philosophy. Return to our practical man and try to imagine him as he moves, as dextrous as he is unconscious, in a totally familiar environment, one that is entirely under his control. But at some point something goes wrong: an element of that environment rebels against the usual manipulations, reacts in an awkward way. For a while our automaton might continue to stolidly apply all his instructions to it; then he will stop, facing a moment of crisis, a void, a functional gap. If he were really an automaton his crisis might last indefinitely, but this individual has other resources too, can take other paths.

E: Maybe the paths that researchers in artificial intelligence have long been looking for, to help true automata overcome their stalemate: their ineptitude with respect to natural language, learning, perception . . .

S: Do you expect that piles of plastic and metal will suddenly begin to think on their own?

R: No, for sure: to think one needs to be invested by the divine breath, as happened to you.

B: Let's try to remain calm. The "automaton" I was referring to, then, can also raise questions, ask why the crisis took place, puzzle over its meaning. It is this act of questioning that constitutes the fact; it is from this point of view that what earlier just happened now becomes a problem, and hence specifically an object of discourse, some*thing* to talk about. The question "why" creates a new functional level, with respect to which *all* that was there before is posited as contrasting and complementary; it requalifies being as subject of a predicate, theme of a rheme, example of a concept, practice of a theory; it establishes a primordial difference, a "before" and an "after" which define not only the transcendental but also the empirical.

E: You should be clear on one point. Is the crisis you are talking about seen from the outside or from the inside? In other words, is it a situation in which ordinary modes of behavior are *objectively* dysfunctional or is it important that they be *experienced* as such?

B: The latter must be the decisive element: questions don't start unless the crisis is felt . . .

E: . . . and sometimes they start when for many the situation would not at all be dysfunctional—some of us are more (self-)critically inclined than others. But then how can the crisis originate the theoretical level, if a *representation* of the crisis is necessary for this origin?

B: You're right, probably my mistake was to stick to an atomistic conception: a single crisis, a single shift in level, a single questioning, a single theorizing. Let's say rather that a certain species of individuals has this behavioral option available (among many): it can break down and go through the process I described. In general this will happen in situations that are truly critical, but not always.

E: If we put it like that, we can also recover what you earlier called the "socio-political aspect" of Angelo's proposals. The breakdown and the questions that follow from it will produce a storytelling, will institute a confrontation and a dialogue with nonbeing, with the possible, with the future. They will bring about ever more deviant, ever more transgressive tales, and sooner or later, by chance, one of those tales might suggest a new, more effective practice. But no single step in this operation contributes to improving our adaptation to the world: only the whole operation (perhaps) makes such a contribution. So it's reasonable to protect ourselves from the potentially destabilizing effect of these steps until we have made *enough* of them to allow for a profitable outcome.

B: That's right. I thought there was a connection, and now I see it clearly.

R: I am glad you do, but I'm still not following. Aside from this very charming but scientifically highly questionable speculative psychology, what are you saying that is new, or different from what I would have said? There is the transcendental, or conceptual, and there is the empirical; the transcendental raises questions on the meaning of the empirical, and so on. You told me a pretty story about how the transcendental and the empirical "are constituted," but the net result is the same.

B: Not quite, Roberto. To begin with, as I said, your position and Angelo's are very similar, but at this point there is already a substantial difference, and his discourse has already been articulated enough to turn against some of its own premises, or maybe just to reinterpret them, change their emphasis, their focus. If earlier the "essence" of the transcendental was to be found in the contrast between facts and concepts, between logic and existence, between words and things, now it is to be found in the check that arrests action, in the perplexity that follows that check, in the astonishment . . .

E: Plato's wonder.

B: Sure, and in a very strong sense. It's not that wonder generated philosophy once and for all, and then the latter continued to exist independently; it's rather that there will be philosophy as long as there is wonder, as long as there are open problems. The connection between philosophy and wonder is not the causal one between a child and its mother, or between a suit and a tailor, but the ontological connection between a table's shape and the table, or between a mother's love and the mother. If you destroy the table you will also destroy its shape, if you kill the mother you will also kill her love, if wonder disappears philosophy disappears too.

R: This image of the philosopher perpetually invaded by the *stupor mundi* is pretty bizarre! Unproductive too, for I imagine that, as a result, our sensitive and delicate friend will forever be twiddling his thumbs.

B: Don't become an activist now; remember that for you there is no possible *action*. At any rate, you got it right: in this perspective there is also an ontological connection between philosophy and inactivity. We have already seen that Angelo justifies the separation between theory and practice in utilitarian terms: philosophers are dangerous, we'd better isolate them, and so on. All this is true, but there is also something else: the fact that questioning and storytelling are *alternatives* to acting, that they are what "one does" *when there is nothing to be done*. They amount to exploring, to shooting in the dark, to trying things out. We are fortunate to have language available as a medium for conducting such experiments, for thus we run fewer risks of burning our fingers and getting hurt, and hence we can understand (and approve of) Angelo's invitation to lock the experimenters in a cage of words. But even if we let them use their hands and feet, or a hammer or an ax, these would still not be actions, practices, they would still not have the repetitive, recognizable character that identifies practices as such, one could not attribute any purposiveness to them . . .

E: Or maybe one could: a "purposiveness without purpose."

B: Maybe. But when one reaches a real purposiveness, when one can make sense of our moving hands and feet, when experimentation has become action, a determinate action, that one and no other, then experimentation is over and philosophy is already elsewhere. Philosophy *is* (essentially) inactivity.

R: Even admitting that this change of emphasis makes some difference, what's the advantage of putting it this way?

B: There is primarily the advantage of a clearer relation between theories and practices—including the *practice of theorizing*. As long as we express ourselves in terms of facts and concepts it's easy to get confused. For example: We can say that the shoemaker's is a practice and the metaphysician's a theory, but what shall we say about science? Angelo would assimilate scientific theories to metaphysics and technological applications to the automatisms of practice, but there is great continuity and integration between the two, not that rigorous, irreparable distinction that seems entailed by the transcendental/empirical dilemma. The scientist operates (or maybe plays) with his symbols at the same times and in the same ways as he operates with his tools (or maybe with the defense budget), and in all these cases his "spirit" is the same: curious and inquiring, jealous of his independence and impatient of any restriction. So how can we justify assigning theoretical weight to some of these activities and not others?

E: Perhaps by referring to the politics of the situation and to its risks. Theory means explanation, understanding, wisdom, and it's best to reserve these honorable appellations for purely symbolic play. Otherwise they might go to your head.

B: OK, but that only tells us why some activities are *denied* theoretical weight, not why some others get it. Indeed it suggests that the "logical space" is not as self-sufficient as our initial formulation led us to believe, that the boundary between theories and practices is a variable one, open to negotiation and debate. And there is also what we are doing right now: raising questions (among other things) about the meaning of philosophy, which involves suspending certain established ways of doing it and experimenting freely with words and sentences, with the possible outcome of establishing new operational structures, a new system of linguistic habits. Clearly we are grappling with a theorization of the current philosophical practice, but what is the relation between this theorization and the practice it theorizes about on the one hand, and the more conventional philosophical theories on the other? Is there perhaps an infinite hierarchy of theories? Or are there two such hierarchies: one of theories and one of practices? Are they connected? And how?

E: Just a moment! Earlier you said that philosophy is not a practice, and now instead . . .

B: That's precisely the problem I am trying to formulate. While you do it, philosophy is not a practice, but when you question its possibility and modes of functioning then certainly you are talking about something, and hence this strange operation has become an object, or maybe philosophy has simply moved: it is no longer what you are talking about, the activity for which you continue by force of habit to use the same name . . .

E: Some would say, "to use it referentially."

B: . . . but it's rather what you do as you talk about it.

S: Now we are totally confused.

B: Yes, and the confusion is due to the wrong emphasis I mentioned earlier. If instead of talking about facts and concepts, thus suggesting an absolute difference, an impassable barrier, we talk about a crisis in a practice, about the shift that follows from it and in turn produces a questioning and a storytelling, everything gets simpler. The crisis and the shift may take place before a computer gone crazy, a sudden increase in the rate of inflation, or maybe the paradox of an activity (like philosophy) which seems entirely unproductive (if not counterproductive) and yet entails heavy social and economic costs. The crisis and the questioning posit a subject of inquiry: to ask, "Why X?", means among other things that, as long as one continues to ask that question, one assumes that X is a fact. But, independently of that crisis and that questioning, there is nothing essentially factual in X, and our next question may arise just from the perplexity into which we are thrown by our having called X a fact, from the reasons we feel we need to give for our move. When that happens we are already facing another crisis, whose object is not so much X as the factuality of X, and which makes us question not so much X as our explanatory activity, our previous theorization, which now, in the new context, before the new shift, the new problem, has already become a theorizing *practice*, a *fact* to be explained.

E: And "questioning" only means interrupting ordinary practices and beginning to "play," and does not necessarily entail using language.

B: Not language as it manifests itself empirically: it's not necessary that anything be spoken or written. But a "transcendental" language may surface whenever a gap opens, in every moment of wonder, and in this language one might be able to raise questions with one's hands rather than one's voice (or pen), and to assign theoretical weight to "free gestures" rather than words. The "factual" nature of the starting point of those gestures would then not be announced, described, but instead physically felt, in the primordial way in which reality can draw our attention, hurting if needed . . .

E: But in this way philosophy loses all its specificity. It is no more "in-activity" than any other form of behavior: it's not yet a practice when one does it, just as cooking and fixing shoes are not (in a world of practices there are no practices), but becomes one as soon as one theorizes about it. What shall we make then of all the talk about an experimenting for its own sake, of which it is impossible to predicate a structure and a goal?

B: You're right, and in some sense there is no answer to your question, not because I don't know it but because an answer cannot even be phrased, because the situation is entirely paradoxical. When you question the fixing of shoes your questioning is theorization, philosophy, inactivity, and this theorization constitutes fixing shoes as an action, a practice; when you question your (earlier) questioning, that questioning of yours—call it "questioning$_1$"—has in turn become a practice and an object of the new questioning—which we can call "questioning$_2$." And so on. So when you *say* that questioning$_1$ is inactivity you are saying something false, because what you are saying now is part of questioning$_2$, where questioning$_1$ is no longer inactivity.

E: There you have the infinite hierarchy you mentioned earlier . . .

R: But didn't you say that philosophy is essentially inactivity, that even if one moves one's hands and mouth while doing it that is not (yet) *doing* anything?

B: And hence I said something I could not say. In terms of the hierarchy I have introduced now, I said (or perhaps only tried to say), "Questioning is inactivity," without subscripts, and this sentence is not so much false as it is meaningless, because there is no point of view from which it could be said, no level of questioning at which it would be legitimate to make such a general statement (so general indeed as to include a reference to itself). It's a bit like in Frege: the concept *horse* is not a concept, because everything we can talk about (including the concept *horse*) is an *object* of discourse, but concepts are categorially different from objects and hence are something that cannot be talked about . . .

E: . . . whereas one can talk about corresponding objects . . .

B: Sure: one can talk about the relevant courses-of-values. In the same way, I can talk about my questioning as an object, about what I do, how I behave, how I move (perhaps figuratively) when I question, and for these movements I might be able in principle to discover a logic, and discovering this logic will mean categorizing them as an action of a certain kind, but I won't be able to do any of this for questioning *as questioning*: precisely its questioning nature will elude me as I devote myself to examining its mortal incarnation.

E: Or perhaps its mortal remains, if I understand you correctly.

B: True: what eludes us when we deal *with* something, for example when we talk about it as a definite action, is its vitality, its capacity to contradict any definition as soon as it's formulated.

S: You seem to be referring to Sartrean subjectivity.

E: But there may be a less dramatic way to put it. Consider the difference between an intentional object and a real one: everything we talk or think about, everything we look for, is an object in the first sense but not always in the second one. Analogously, we might say that philosophy is an intentional or possible practice which will never be a real one, never acquire that repetitive and recognizable character which is required for it to be real. This distinction would allow us to avoid all absurdities and talk without problems about what is specifically philosophical.

B: Your proposal is ingenious, but runs up against the intrinsic limitations of the notion of possibility. To speak of an object (or a practice) as possible means to bet that *it could be real*; so if one proves that it cannot be, the bet is lost and all that previous talk is shown to be meaningless, however credible it might have seemed at the time. According to Angelo, remember, an intentional object is only a manner of speaking, not another kind of object. Therefore to regard philosophy as a practice means to commit oneself to constituting it as a specific, definite practice, a real one, with all the attending risks, and to conclude that this reality is inaccessible means to acknowledge the failure of one's commitment.

E: Surely that is a "strong" way of conceiving intentionality . . .

B: . . . which on the other hand has often been used to neutralize conflicts and construct a cosy, sweetish limbo where one can enjoy "contradictory objects" and other nonsense.

E: In conclusion, the distinction between transcendental and empirical is not so much one of scope as one of role, and the same roles can be assigned to different actors . . .

B: . . . and will in turn constitute scopes, but different scopes in different circumstances, facing different problems . . .

E: Not entirely different, though: they are still always examples of the same kind of problem, though it may be impossible to *say* what kind it is.

B: It's impossible unless one submits to paradox, to self-referentiality, to meaninglessness. But here we are speaking freely . . .

R: Too much so, it seems to me.

B: . . . and hence we can accept such questionable means of expression, we can come out of the complicated hierarchy we have put together and speak about it from the outside, speak *of* that hierarchy.

E: After all, that's precisely what a philosopher ought to do, Angelo would say: violate conventions and rules.

B: Good, so speaking freely I will say that you're right, that in a way it's always the same problem: that of rationalizing the unknown, of weaving a web of comforting, reassuring words all around it, of telling stories that have already happened ("Once upon a time . . .", "Statistical evidence proves that . . .", "On the basis of our experiences . . .") and thus acquiring at least an appearance of control, since true control, the one that needs no words, that moves with blind, adamant confidence, is not there yet—or no longer.

Three

ENRICO: Are you saying that according to Angelo practices rule out language?

BERTOLDO: What I am saying, perhaps, is that they rule out its *meaning*. Some language (understood empirically) will often surface among them: among the various things one does one will also utter words, one will say for example, "Bring me a slab," or, "I want five apples," causing predictable reactions in the audience. But none of this will have a meaning yet. Meaning arises when automatisms come to a stop, when what earlier just happened becomes an object of puzzlement. Then appears a discourse *about* that object, a discourse *that speaks of* that object, where that object enters as a referent, as designated; then language becomes meaningful.

E: And hence becomes language, for a language is not made only of sounds and conditioned reflexes. Otherwise, thunder would be speaking a language when it's heard from far away and urges us to hurry home.

B: You are right: I realize that from this point of view much of what we empirically call language is only that by courtesy—or by contagion. In a proper (if you will, transcendental) sense there is language only when there is meaning and hence only when a crisis opens up.

ROBERTO: But aren't you getting confused? Shouldn't you say instead that in such moments of crisis *you*, as an epistemic subject, raise *the problem* of meaning? Once that problem is solved, you realize that meaning and language are also present elsewhere, in situations that are not critical, in the flattest normality, even in sentences like "Bring me a slab."

B: It's always a question of emphasis, Roberto. I might happen to think what you say, but even then I will remember that it's only because I experienced a moment of crisis that I ended up speaking of meaning, that the meaning attributed to situations that are *not* critical has been attributed to them only for the sake of generality, so these situations have meaning for extrinsic reasons and may lose it if I change my theory.

R: They can't *lose it*: I may *think* that they lose it. If something has meaning, I don't see how my personal vicissitudes could change that.

E: Once again, it's clear that you are on opposite sides of the fence: for one of you what is foundational is metaphysics and for the other it's epistemology.

B: I would prefer to put it in terms of objects and experiences . . .

STEFANO: Let's try not to stray too far. We were speaking of the relation between practices and language.

B: OK. According to Angelo, the conceptual locus of meaning is in the reader or hearer—say in general in the public—and more precisely in the public insofar as it tries to explain what it's witnessing. These statements are often misunderstood as trivially (that is, empirically) psychological, or even worse as pure and simple linguistic legislation: "From now on, the word 'meaning' must be understood thus and so." But in my opinion there is something more serious at stake here, though it's difficult to formulate it clearly. To begin with, everyone can be an audience to himself and hence the essence of this process is not to be found in a difference of individuals. It is rather to be found in the attention with which we turn to what crystallizes precisely through that attention and becomes a *topic* of attention and discussion, in the duplicity thus created between the questioning agency and its object, even when they happen to be the same, in the intrusiveness, the thickness, the heavy, brutal factuality with which suddenly the object constituted as such imposes itself and asks for a reason, for *its own* reason, demands the beginning of a search for its own meaning—that is: the beginning of an experimental use of linguistic resources, the interruption of an automatic and unreflective correlation between words and (other) things and the exordium of words left to themselves, words that refer to other words, that find in other words their temporary legitimation, that chase each other in a definitional and narrative play which is supposed to clarify them but obscures them instead, since only one true "clarification" is possible, one "successful" outcome, and that's the end of play, the return of the automatism. Some *other* time we might perhaps raise the problem of all this, and reason about it in terms of a practice of articulation where the illusion of meaning is given only, for an instant, by the resonance of familiarity; but then discourse and its meaning will already have moved—they will be the discourse *of* this articulation, and of *its* meaning.

E: So meaning and language originate within the theoretical operation of questioning.

B: Better still: this operation simultaneously constitutes language and its object. Questioning the meaning of experience, of any experience, establishes its objectivity and at the same time posits a linguistic episode as an a posteriori commentary on it, as an exploration of the conditions of possibility of a *fact* that qualifies as irremediably earlier and thus creates an irremediable dialectic between earlier and later. It makes this experience be, in other words, since it brings out the gap that is necessary for it to become the objective of an intentionality. Hearing Angelo, one might even think that in this gap, in this multiplication of planes, must be found the origin of time as the "dimension of experience"—of its logical structure, I mean, not its qualitative content: the logical structure of a linear succession, of a rhythm, of a series.

E: Experience then is something that has *already* happened?

B: Yes, as long as "already" is understood logically: its *chrono*logical nature will then result from an empirical realization of this transcendental condition.

E: And even this "then" must be understood logically.

B: That's right. In logical terms, therefore, experience (or, perhaps better, *an* experience) is something whose being is not (any longer) an issue and about which one can speak, something to which, in order to speak about it, one must deny the possibility of further developments, something one must reduce to those dead remains, those crystallized residues we were earlier hinting at. And because even speaking of it is a potential experience, a possible future experience, and because this process can be repeated indefinitely, we need an infinite line, a dimension, on which to organize discourse and locate all its "objects."

E: I see what you mean when you speak of difficulties of expression. And it's not just that these ideas are very complicated: there also seem to be violent tensions between different needs, different parts of the structure. Consider this point, for example: Angelo often speaks of the transgressive character of the confabulating operation, and you too just reminded us that it's best for everyone if the confabulation is limited to language. At the same time, though, he also speaks of this operation as a reassuring one, which fills with an avalanche of words a destabilizing operational void, an implicit threat to our integration and functionality. How shall we understand this contrast? Do we need the revolution to sleep soundly?

B: Remember what we said earlier—what you yourself forced me to spell out clearly—concerning the distinction between an "atomistic" level and a global one. By adopting this transgressive and revolutionary attitude it's perhaps possible to reach a state of calm, but not because every step takes us toward that state. On the contrary, every step takes us elsewhere and a good deal of bad faith is needed to think that we are going in the right direction—a bad faith which may ultimately prove precious. But let's take things in order. Suppose that a situation X involves an operational stalemate: our practices break down, our tools prove useless, we no longer know how to move, a crisis opens up. There might follow the posing of a problem; we might ask, "Why X?"—or, if you prefer, "What does X mean?" By asking this question we are looking for an escape from our embarrassment: an answer will bring relief, fill every lacuna, draw a map of the situation, and make everything add up. Such at least is the ideology, but how far it is from the real nature of the operation! What is an answer to the question, "Why X?", if not a reference to some Y which *is not* X and which in turn, with as much legitimacy, generates the question, "Why Y?" And what does a chain of questions of this kind produce if not a growing forgetfulness of X, an ever more conspicuous drift away from *its* reality? It's certainly possible that, by playing like this, we will put a mechanism in motion that helps us overcome our embarrassment, and there may be no other way of proceeding in this impasse, but even if the thing works it's not for the reason one thinks. *It's not true* (as people think) that slowly but surely we get closer to a solution and an understanding; what we do instead is slowly but surely *get farther* from any solution and understanding, and then suddenly, in a casual and discontinuous way, our path takes us far enough to create a new, different possibility of effectiveness. Then the problem is solved, but not because we finally understood or because understanding makes a difference, not because any single thing we did was useful. It was useful to do things like that, and perhaps it was also useful to think that doing things like that was useful, if it helped make us do them.

E: You seem to propose an implicit solution for the paradox of analysis: an answer to the question, "What is X?", will always bring out something different from X, and if this operation ever proves valuable in dealing with X it's only because it has contributed to reorganizing the whole operational field, including X.

B: Well said! The ideal of an analysis that resolves its object into something identical to itself—that ideal on which so much philosophical inquiry is based—is a purely mystifying one. Analysis is nothing but a way (or better, an excuse) to digress.

E: Perhaps it's just this capacity to digress that an automaton needs in order to become "intelligent"; perhaps we should teach it our ideological duplicity.

B: Perhaps: we should teach it to transgress orders, *our* orders, and to do unpredictable and foolish things. We should teach it the play (and gamble) of "aimless" experimentation. But such a requirement is at cross-purposes with any criterion of functionality: what we expect from a computer is that it do what it's told, and hence it would be absurd to let it disobey (or, even worse, to advise it to disobey).

E: More than absurd, terrifying. The nightmare of HAL could become a tragic reality.

S: In conclusion, gentlemen, it doesn't seem that your facts took you very far. Or, at least, it doesn't seem that you were able to exclude from the range of facts things that everyone recognizes—everyone who doesn't practice our strange profession, I mean. I certainly don't want to deny that a large part of my behavior is determined by events not belonging to me. If you, Roberto, were to suddenly appear before me—especially you—I could not help being startled; if someone overtakes me and cuts me off I can't help swerving right; if a fly buzzes in my ear I can't help shooing it. We have indefinitely many reflexes and irresistible reactions, but we have something else too. There are cases, few cases perhaps but also the most important ones—both because the most serious things are decided then and because they put us in contact with the most essential core of our personality, with what distinguishes us from machines and animals . . .

E: Up until now, maybe. When machines get smarter . . .

S: . . . cases in which we are able to escape the tyranny of automatism, to stop and deliberate about our actions, to evaluate the pros and cons, and finally to decide on the basis of what we really want, suspending with this act of freedom any influences of the environment, of our character, and of our past history.

R: I take note of this declaration and I don't deny that it agrees with common sense, with the ideas of those who don't practice "our strange profession." But our strange profession consists of verifying the legitimacy of ideas—the common and the less common ones, our own and those of others. And in terms of legitimacy what you say is highly questionable. For example, you call the result of deliberation an "act of freedom," but what do you mean by that? What content do you give to the word "freedom"?

S: That no one forced me to act like this: neither an external agency nor an internal automatism. By inhibiting any unconsidered reaction, I let my reason speak, my will.

R: Come on, Stefano, let's not trivialize everything! Sure, from a phenomenological point of view *you feel* free, *you don't experience* any constraint, *it seems to you* that you are not reacting automatically, but shall we accept these impressions of yours without testing them at all? Shall we say that you are free whenever you feel free? We must move from the empirical data to concepts, from experience to a logical demonstration of possibility. And in this regard I believe there are only two ways you can go. You can say that being free is having the capacity to do otherwise, that you are not only running but have also freely chosen to run if it would be possible for you *not* to run. Then, however, all your deliberations will give you no support. At most, these detours will prove that you are subject to conflicting influences and that some time is needed before the strongest of them asserts itself. If there were an absolute balance among two or more of these springs you would behave like Buridan's ass and starve to death, but this certainly would not prove your freedom. Despite all we have said so far and the many complications (gratuitous ones, I think) ventured by our friends, the statement that every event has a cause—that is, that for every event e_1 there exists an event e_2 (or a class of events e_2, e_3 . . .) which precedes e_1 and of which e_1 is a necessary consequence—is much better confirmed than its negation and hence makes a much more credible claim on our assent. But if we assent to this statement then your "choice" to do A rather than B, whatever may have been at the time your sensation of freedom from any constraint, was entirely necessitated. *You could not have done otherwise* and hence, according to this conception of freedom, *were not free.* Or you could say that being free is acting under no *outside* influence, in the way Spinoza and Leibniz (among others) thought of God as free: not that He could ever do otherwise—in every case, He couldn't do anything but the good, indeed the greatest possible good—but no one else forced Him to do what He did, it followed inexorably from the laws of His own nature. Well, in this case too you're in bad shape, because you're not God, which in particular means: you're not infinite. Not only is your "free" choice to run a necessary consequence of something else X, but X is a necessary consequence of Y and Y of Z and so on, and since you're not infinite at some point in this series you will find yourself outside the spatiotemporal scope of your life, forced to attribute your running to something that does not belong to you, for which you can't be responsible, which you can't have chosen. So, however you put it, you must conclude that your impression of freedom when you deliberate and decide is fallacious, just like an impression of seeing a unicorn or hearing the sirens. In one case as in the others, "vivid" does not imply "true."

E: Your conclusion might not be so inevitable, Roberto. There is at least one other conception of freedom you did not deal with, the Humean one: being free is doing what one wants, which does not exclude that one is somehow necessitated to do it. If I want to run and do run, I will run freely, and any reflection on my genetic heritage, my family, my education, or the examples I was set—however interesting in other respects—will be entirely irrelevant to this issue. The only relevant question, concerning an action A done by x, will be, "Did x want to do A?", and if the answer is, "Yes," then x did A freely, period.

B: Sure, and this conception must be taken seriously, in view of how important it is for our juridical structure. Think of the distinction between first-degree murder and manslaughter: independently of the victim's death, and even of how atrocious this death was, the defendant's degree of responsibility (and hence of freedom) is decided on the basis of what he *wanted* . . .

E: . . . and when the defense lawyer tries to convince us that the defendant, though perhaps he wanted to act in a certain way, was not free because he could not act otherwise—because, for example, his crime was an "expression" of a certain social status, of certain (perverse) cultural mechanisms, or of a (more or less temporary) mental illness—the debate centers in essence on which notion of freedom we should accept.

R: But aren't you just moving the problem back one step? OK, x wanted to do A, but was this wanting of his free?

E: No, just a moment, you are the one who is moving the problem. I am not interested in whether x's *wanting* to run is free: we are not speaking of this. I am interested in whether *his running* is free, and this *is* free if he wanted to run. In order to know whether his wanting to run is free, one should ask whether x wanted *to want to run*, but even if the answer to that question were, "No," nothing negative would follow concerning the first question.

R: All right. So let's take a classic example. I hypnotize you and tell you, "When you wake up, go close the window and forget everything I told you." You wake up, look around worried, manifesting a growing embarrassment, and finally muster all your courage and go close the window. I ask you, "Why did you do that?", and you answer, "Because I was getting cold." Question: is this a case in which you wanted to close the window? So is it a case in which you closed it *freely*?

S: Clearly not: it only seemed to him that he wanted to close it, but he didn't really want it. Someone else did.

R: There is no doubt that someone else did, but how can he deny that he did too *and hence* that he acted freely—in his "Humean" sense of freedom? On what basis can we decide that someone wants something, if not the subjective sensation that accompanies wanting—a sensation that in this case is clearly present?

E: I believe that your rhetorical questions have answers, Roberto, and that the situation is not as desperate as you suggest. Suppose that I love you, that I want your good, that in all circumstances I do my best to make things work out for you. Then some day a cruel enemy of ours administers to me, without my knowledge, a drug that makes every human being hate his neighbor. Under the influence of the drug I walk with you to your garage and, while you are busy around the shelves, I get caught by an irresistible urge to destroy you. Thus, without further ado, I start the car and squash you against the wall like a roach.

S: Jesus Christ!

B: A suggestive hypothesis, and a troublesome one. Come to think of it, what's the difference between the drug you're talking about and what the media feed us every day as advertisements? That drug too makes us hate our neighbor, since in order to create the necessary dissatisfaction—which will then be "discharged" by buying deodorants and detergents—it constantly forces us to compare ourselves with unreal models of physical and domestic perfection, thus making us feel our lives, our bodies, and our relationships as contemptible, and causing a frightening desire for revenge against all those who seem closer to the fascinating and formidable models. No wonder our suburban monster watched TV up to eight hours a day!

S: What would you propose, then? To apologize to him and send him back home, maybe with a fifty-inch screen as a gift?

E: Don't get excited, Stefano: no one here is proposing anything, at most we are trying to understand. Returning to my example, can we say that *I wanted* to kill Roberto? First of all, this is a question with a subject ("Did *I* want to kill him?"), and hence we must find not only an act of will but also the character to which it belongs. Is it so obvious that it was I who wanted, just because this irrepressible impulse crossed my brain and moved my body? But then I should also ascribe to myself every episode in which I want (or rather, in which I seem to want, in which it seems to me *I* want) something in a dream or a delirium, and ordinarily I don't do that. And why don't I do it? Because such a self-ascription involves an assessment of the consistency of what I did, of what I apparently *wanted* to do, with what *else* I want to do, with the more general structure of my desires, with my longer-range plans. If there is no such consistency, the suspicion arises that I didn't really want, not (necessarily) because there was no *wanting*, nor because there wasn't *someone* who wanted, but because that someone was not me, *couldn't* have been me. If I had established that your presence was generally undesirable and had carefully orchestrated your disappearance, one could recognize me in what happened, but as things are one can't: as things are, that event, that guilt do not belong to me, it wasn't I who wanted them, and hence they don't issue from my freedom.

B: It's like saying that there must be some method to being evil.

E: As indeed to "being" anything . . .

R: Very interesting, but you certainly wandered far from your first formulation. That one, at least, was clear and precise, and therefore easy to attack; now you have clouded it to the point of making it virtually unfalsifiable. How will you decide *in concreto* what belongs to an agent? How long will you have to look in his history to establish that an act is consistent with his "longer-range plans"?

E: I don't think I owe you an answer, Roberto, since you are arbitrarily raising the standards of acceptability for the positions of others well beyond the level you consider adequate for your own. I told you in general, in principle, how things could go, and you reply by asking for a decision procedure. Tell me then on the basis of what procedure you decided that the principle of causality "is much better confirmed than its negation"? Earlier Bertoldo gently raised some doubts on this article of faith of yours: you let it go for a while by defending a position of simple "categorial determinacy" ("It's the sort of thing that is either true or false, though we are not able to establish which") and then, as soon as you could, charged back with a more technical formulation. But, despite the technicalities, the problems are still there. The logical structure of the principle of causality is, "For every x there is a y such that y causes x," and the structure of its negation is, "There is an x such that, for every y, y does not cause x." Therefore, since both the principle and its negation are statements of universal import and the ranges of both x and y are potentially infinite, not only a conclusive verification but even a statistical confirmation of the one or the other appears entirely hopeless. It makes sense to cite statistical data to support a hypothesis concerning the dangers of a smoking habit, but attempting to "confirm" the principle of causality (or its negation) would be like thinking that after a number of positive examples a mathematical conjecture might become "truer." In conclusion, you too have done nothing but tell us a story, a plausible one perhaps but nothing more than a story, and you can't ask others for decision procedures.

B: This is an outcome Angelo would have liked a lot.

E: Yes, I know; for him, philosophy reduces to literature. I am not in total agreement: I would distinguish between the large narrative constructions—the big systems—whose correctness it would be absurd to try to prove, and the specific theses that can be advanced and proved within such systems. But, at any rate, I would like to know what "story" he tells about this freedom we have been discussing so heatedly.

B: I would too: his remarks in this regard are rather fragmentary, and it's not at all clear to me that they can be organized in a coherent discourse. If you want, I'll try to bring them out one at a time, and maybe together we will be able to capture their general sense.

R: If indeed they do make sense!

S: Sure, Roberto: only your "scientific" formulations make sense. Except when they prove themselves giants with feet of clay.

E: It seems clear that our conversation has reached a deadlock. So come on, Bertoldo: it's about time to introduce a new element.

Four

BERTOLDO: It's hard to understand how new Angelo's position is. I have heard him say many of the things you guys have been saying, at one time or another, but the spirit of his remarks was undeniably different.

ENRICO: Perhaps what was different was the point of view; perhaps we should begin with that "Copernican revolution" which seems the keystone of all his developments.

B: You're right, let's begin there. So our conceptual foundation is no longer the notion of an object but that of an experience: objects must be reached, "constructed," along a philosophical—or, equivalently, a narrative—path.

E: Which entails, if I am not mistaken, that one will be able to say more, and more interesting things, about objects than in the traditional context.

B: Yes. The pre-Copernican, or transcendental realist, paradigm will find it natural to articulate other themes. For example, once an experience is defined as a certain property or state of a certain kind of object, classifying experiences and providing conceptual conditions that establish their veridicality, their "correspondence" with the world, will be a program of great interest. Epistemology will present itself as an obvious way of investing intellectual resources. From the post-Copernican or

transcendental idealist point of view, on the other hand, there will be little to say about experiences as such, but there will be a lot to say about
the world. "Being in the world," which for traditional reflection was a
primitive notion, to be liquidated (when it was considered at all) with
more or less tautological clauses—"to exist in a primary sense," "to be
the bearer of properties"—will now potentially become the topic of a sophisticated and informative analysis, of an intricate "story" . . .

E: . . . like Heideggerian ontology . . .

B: . . . which from this point of view can be seen not as an epochal
watershed and a "return" to presocratic wisdom, but rather as an inevitable step in the surfacing of the range of issues proper to the new
paradigm.

E: Which might not be so new after all. All that talk about feminism,
or the feminine . . .

B: OK, but if we do want to talk about precedents there is no need to
go back to the very dawn of our civilization. The confrontation and contrast between the two paradigms—which, I admit without reservation, it
is purely conventional to call "old" and "new"—runs through the whole
history of philosophy, sometimes getting entangled in extremely significant dialectical knots. Think of the perennial enigma represented by the
ontological argument for the existence of God, and of the dramatic, fundamental oscillation reflected in that enigma: is our thinking and speaking *of objects* or are objects, essentially, *of thought* and *of discourse?* One
has to choose between these two approaches, but if one gets confused
and maintains both, the rabbit comes out of the hat: to speak of something makes it an object in the second sense and hence, given the connection between existence and objectivity in the first sense, makes it an
existent too.

E: I understand, and it seems that your analysis explains a central aspect of the debate on this argument, that is, the fact that it's hard to re-
strict it to an argument for the existence *of God.*

B: Exactly. From Gaunilo on, the problem has been always the same:
How can we avoid a generalized use of this trick, or better of this illusion? How can we prevent an indiscriminate multiplication of "ontological proofs"?

E: To return to freedom, one will have to establish first of all *who* is
free, find room for the subject.

B: Yes, and on this theme too there will be a sharp contrast. For the
realist tradition, the subject is a particular *object*, characterized by particular properties. It will be necessary to establish what these properties

are, but insofar as we are dealing with an object, its existence and self-identity will not be in question: they will automatically follow from the "place" assigned to it in logical space. The only true alternative here will be the one—pursued by Hume, for example, and (sometimes) by Russell—of denying it this place, of describing the world without any reference to it, of demoting it to the status of a convenient abbreviation for a "deep" reality that excludes it. For transcendental idealism, however, the situation is quite different. We can admit that every experience has a subject insofar as it is lived from a determinate point of view, insofar as it presents itself as expressing a determinate perspective . . .

E: Pardon my interruption, but the possibility of eliminating the subject seems to be present in this paradigm too. Sure, we have a tendency to prefix an "I think" to every experience, and hence to qualify it as ours, but is this a necessity? And if it *is* a necessity, perhaps a linguistic one, how can we avoid its reduction to a simple, insubstantial formality? What difference would it make if, instead of "I'm hungry" or "I see a table," we said "There is hunger" or "A table is seen"?

B: Well put, Enrico, and this wonderfully pointed question invites me to confess a failure. As you mentioned earlier, I've been listening to Angelo for years, and for years I forced him and forced *myself* to reformulate his theses and his arguments in an orderly manner: this follows from that, and that follows from the other, and so on. He, of course, has always rebelled against my logical restrictions. You know how he is: a constant whirlwind of ideas, of suggestions, of provocations. And just as naturally, I kept thinking that I was right: that my way of speaking was the only possible one, the only way of *saying* something instead of uttering random sounds. But with time my conviction grew weak, and I began to suspect that my project was impracticable, that what I wanted to say, or help him say, *could not* be said, because of the intrinsic limitations of saying itself, because saying forces us to a before and an after, whereas the object of our saying is an organic totality, in which all elements hang together, and even just beginning somewhere is already a cause of strain.

E: But you yourself said that this linearity, this temporality, is essential to philosophy . . .

B: . . . and hence puts it in the unfortunate condition of being constitutionally inadequate, inevitably defective, perpetually in search of an ideal formulation which eludes it, which must elude it.

ROBERTO: What low-level romanticism! All language is linear, not just philosophical language. Even when you describe a room you must cite

some things first and others later, whereas in the room things are present all at the same time, and yet we hear no childish lamentations over
the impossibility of an "ideal formulation" of the room.

B: You're right, Roberto, but there is a profound difference between
the two cases. The room exists (or, I should say, is conceived as existent)
even if no one talks about it; philosophy, on the other hand, is constituted precisely by talking. Its "organic totality" has a purely imaginary
nature. Its "space" is painstakingly "posited" through the operation of
describing it and hence—given the linear nature of this operation—will
never exist "all at the same time."

R: Instead of crying about these results you should turn them around
to prove the absurdity of your position. Why should philosophy be constituted by talking? Philosophy describes a conceptual space which is
just as real as the physical one, and just as independent of any linguistic
operation.

B: And this clearly metaphorical use of the word "space" does not
trouble you at all?

R: Why should it? Wasn't it you who insisted, a while ago, that it's
possible to "feel" the moral command not to murder with the same empirical vividness as the red color of a pen? Wasn't that a metaphor?

B: I was taking a dialectical position then: I wanted to emphasize the
weakness of your rigid categorial distinction between facts and values,
and show you how many "values" your "facts" are drenched in, how
many choices made necessary only by habit are hidden behind that distinction. I certainly did not intend to support a positive thesis; I even
said that I don't regard myself as someone who has theses to defend.

E: Now however you are developing one, even if it's not your own,
and I'm curious to see how it will go. So let's leave aside Roberto's
"naive" realism and return to ourselves, or better to your difficulty.

B: OK. So I was making a desperate effort to start ab ovo, in the most
general possible terms. I spoke of objects, of experiences, and I was beginning to speak of subjects when your question exposed me, got me on
the ropes, ridiculed my pretense and presumption of order. For the only
way to answer it, from Angelo's point of view, is by calling into play
much more complex structures, at which it would have been logically
"fitting" to arrive later, hence which force us in some sense to put the
cart before the horse.

E: What structures are those?

B: I am talking about the deviant and controversial practice of questioning, of challenging the legitimacy of something, of looking for a rea-

son. I am talking about systematic transgression, about the drift that transgression sets up, about its going elsewhere, its revolting against the tyranny of what exists, what is automatic, what is functional. In short, I am talking once again about philosophy, which, with the pretext of explaining and reassuring, of resolving and integrating, instead ends up constantly violating our expectations, problematizing all that is obvious, criticizing every authority and tradition. According to Angelo philosophy posits *in fact*—and it's a different matter whether or not one acquires consciousness of this positing, whether or not it in turn becomes a possible theme of inquiry and analysis—it posits a level different from the one where everything existent is located, where the world is, a level of equal dignity to that of the world, a level from which the world can be judged and possibly found at fault: a point of view, a perspective . . .

E: You mean a subject.

B: Sure, but not only in the trivial linguistic terms you were (reasonably) afraid everything could come down to. It's certainly a triviality that we say, "I'm hungry," instead of, "There is hunger," but it's not a triviality that there is, indeed that there must be, space for both these modes of expression, and for their difference. The distinction between subjective and objective, between the "I think" and the real, has a precise function: it makes room for the possibility of going *beyond* the real, in the name of a need, of a desire to change it, to turn it into something else, something "better," even if at the moment one doesn't know how.

E: I believe I understand, and I realize how subtly interconnected all these themes are. Your remarks about philosophy already reminded Stefano earlier of some extreme formulations of the free and "negative" character of subjectivity—existentialist formulations, for the sake of a label. Now the synergism between philosophy and subjectivity becomes something more than a mysterious resonance: one begins to identify its laws. The "ideological" goal of philosophy is the rational reconstruction of the world, but the practice expressed by this ideology does nothing but systematically shift the attention elsewhere, toward what is not (yet) world. Analogously, the ideological goal of the subject is to understand reality and appropriate it, but its practice consists in contesting that reality, in opposing it, in imposing its own values on it . . .

B: . . . and in reducing it to one of many possible "constructs" *on the basis of the subject's experience*, thus disavowing its brutal, opaque immediacy, disowning its pretense of priority . . .

E: Are you talking about the doctrine of privileged access?

B: In a way yes, but we must be careful. When it declares its original character, its foundational role within a rational reconstruction of what happens, when it asserts that nothing can ever get the upper hand over what directly belongs to it, when it excludes its self-perception from the range of fallible experiences, the critical subject is speaking at the theoretical level proper to it. At the practical level external reality will always win, because such reality *is* (or at least includes) the set of practices . . .

E: So we must be clear that the privilege of this access and the priority that follows from it are transcendental.

B: Yes: we must be clear that we are not concerned here with empirical knowledge. From an empirical point of view, I can know any one of you, and in general any element of the public world, with as much certainty as I know myself, indeed even greater certainty because all of you are definite objects for me in a way in which I will never be (for myself). But when the *concept* of knowledge is in question, it becomes important (politically important, I would say) to assert the priority of that experience one has decided to attribute to the subject—in a word, the priority of *privacy*—to everything that we acknowledge as existent. It's important because it amounts to announcing the unexhausted need for an invocation of what is not but does not for that reason matter less—indeed not being proposes itself as a theoretical guarantee for all that is, since by opposing it it qualifies it, defines it, makes it possible to assign it a nature.

E: The theme of need (or, as you said earlier, of desire) is also one we could do a lot of digging into; sooner or later, I am sure, we will have to return to it. This conversation really has a disturbing tendency to spread all over the map, and I understand your dissatisfaction. If I were you, however, I would not let myself be discouraged. Your demand for clarity is certainly useful: it will not make us write an unassailable treatise, which no one would read anyway, but it will make us discuss matters with as much rigor as possible, and illuminate every time as much of the road as we can see—or construct.

B: Thank you for the sympathy but, believe me, getting discouraged is part of the game too. Let us admit then that experience has a subject . . .

STEFANO: Wait a minute: I am not ready to admit anything at all. It's OK to attribute freedom, negation, and transgression to the subject, but do you mean to say that subjectivity is nothing else? Didn't you forget the most important thing, its most properly defining feature? What does the contrast between subjects and (other) objects reduce to if not the fact that the former are *conscious* and the latter are not? You speak of privileged access in transcendental terms, but how do you deal with the *empirical* fact that the subject is identified through the consciousness it has of itself?

B: We—or rather, Angelo would—deal with it by denying that it is a fact. Subjectivity is primarily unconscious.

S: Now don't start playing with words, Freud-style. Even if you decide to use the term "subjectivity" to designate something else, it is still true that there is a radical difference between conscious and unconscious structures.

B: It may be true for you, but not for the "revolutionary" point of view we are exploring. As we said already, it's a matter of reorganizing the logical space, so one can expect that some differences that used to be considered radical no longer will be, and that others will become so, that some "substantial" aggregates will break up . . .

E: Do you mean that *conscious* will no longer be a natural kind?

B: Precisely. Consciousness will be a function, like drinking or sleeping, and just as there are no "drinking beings" or "sleeping beings" . . .

S: And what would be the function of this simple representation, repetition of experience? And why should subjects be the ones to have it, perhaps together with many unconscious functions? Or is that a mistake too: is consciousness to be extended to boats and boots?

B: I don't think it's a mistake: the connection between subjectivity and consciousness is certainly a very close one. But it's not an analytic, definitional connection: there is rather an interesting and complicated story to be told about it.

E: If I understand where you are going, since subjectivity was defined as a form of transgression, such transgression makes consciousness necessary.

B: You understand perfectly, with one qualification. If consciousness is a function, it is the necessity of this function that we can prove. Why the function should be performed by something that has the qualitative features of my conscious life I won't be able to explain—indeed I would say that this is not even a philosophical problem, since philosophy always abstracts from the qualitative nature of experience.

E: It would be like saying that it's not a philosophical problem why the color green should make exactly the impression it makes on me.

B: Right; and notice that this strategy lets us avoid idle questions concerning how far your conscious life is (qualitatively) comparable to mine, and concentrate on the task they both serve.

E: So let us concentrate on that. What task is it?

B: A repressive one.

S: Here goes Freud again!

B: And not by chance, for in Freud we can find, though not always explicitly, many useful conceptual tools for the articulation of the new paradigm. But Freud is not the only one to point out that consciousness has a lot in common with attention, and what is attention if not a control mechanism? If subversive elements circulate in a country, one will first of all have to pay attention to them, keep them constantly in focus.

E: So consciousness is a police operation?

B: I'd rather say an intelligence operation. One will have to infiltrate the conspirators and make their secrets accessible. The transgression that constitutes subjectivity works best when it's not being observed: to make it conscious means to open a channel of communication with the outside, with the realm of what is existent and repetitive, and traditional, and already seen—that realm against which transgression works.

E: That would explain why creativity is often unconscious.

B: Not just "often," but necessarily: there is a constitutional opposition between exploration and awareness, a constant dialectic between thinking of something new and realizing that one is thinking of it.

S: So my consciousness would not really be mine!

B: Only in the sense in which your prison cell can be yours, or your straitjacket.

S: You can talk like that because you are so desperately stuck with an intellectualist view of human nature! With consciousness you associate thoughts, words, and concepts, and then it's easy for you to put it in terms of secret societies and more or less delirious reform plans. But suppose now that the police have caught one of these revolutionaries of yours and are giving him the third-degree: don't you think he would be conscious of the pain he feels? And in what sense would *this* consciousness play the game of "public" power?

E: Yes: Angelo always speaks of pain in a figurative way. He speaks of a check, of instability, of a crisis, but what would he say about a toothache?

B: To be honest, I just don't know what he would say about it. I wish he were here to answer for himself. But I agree that his paradigmatic examples of pain are psychological: it is from such examples—from anxiety, say—that one must begin if one wants to understand a toothache, not vice versa.

S: I'd like to know how.

E: The reference to Freud may be helpful. Anxiety is a consequence (or a signal) of a fragmentation of personality, and personality is constituted starting from the body . . .

B: . . . which is certainly a public object.

E: That's right, and at this point it seems to me that your earlier remarks should be revised. Consciousness is not an independent control function for subjectivity. Rather, this function is performed by a complex structure: personality, in fact, understood as a coherent system, a definite *thing*. When transgression has been objectified into a specific individual then it has been bridled, seized, and to keep it that way various strategies will be used. Attention is one, to be sure, but not the only one: there is also a vigorous negative reaction against any threat to that integrity . . .

B: . . . a threat which is ultimately in the subject's interest.

S: You aren't going to tell me now that it's in the subject's interest to get hurt!

B: Not the empirical subject's, but that one is such a mess of different influences and projects that it's practically impossible to organize it without a transcendental "guide." On the path we are trying to follow, the origin of the subject is to be found in the negation of every structure, hence if a structure is imposed on the subject itself that must be in the interest of what is *not* subject. *As a subject*, the subject must have a tendency to destroy the structure . . .

E: . . . and pain as an alarm signal will be working for the structure, and for what exists.

S: But what structure can a screaming newborn have? How can external reality have already conditioned it? Will you end up speaking of intrauterine conditioning?

B: Why not? As long as it's not understood as *social* conditioning. Certainly the newborn has a structure, and this structure exists, belongs to external reality, rebels like every other part of that reality against any threat of destruction—following some kind of biological program, or conditioning. But that's not to say that the newborn has a subjectivity, hence that its screams must somehow be associated with it.

E: Your example seems to turn against you.

S: I don't believe so. I can think that subjectivity is born precisely out of elementary experiences like this one, but what can *you* think? Why should the newborn have consciousness of pain, that is, have the spies operating in it, *before* it has a subjectivity, hence before it has what the spies should be spying on? And what about a fly whose wings are pulled off: do you want to say that it feels nothing or that it too has a tendency to transgression?

B: Probably Angelo would say that it feels something but is not conscious of it, just as we "see" the road as we drive home, and behave in a way that is perfectly appropriate to what we see, without realizing it, while perhaps devoting all our attention to something else—who knows?—to speaking with a friend, to reflecting on a philosophical problem.

E: Come to think of it, we can even be unaware of having a toothache . . .

B: In fact, we might even (obscurely) *want* to be unaware of it. Becoming aware of it means admitting that there is a problem, that our structure is in danger, that something must be done about it. In short, *feeling* is an ambiguous concept: in some sense I felt a toothache even before I became conscious of it . . .

E: . . . hence pain is not necessarily connected with consciousness . . .

B: I believe pain is, because pain is an ideal, cultural, linguistic structure—in the sense of transcendental language, I mean, not of the empirical one: of the language that comes up whenever life presents itself (to our attention) as a problem. The toothache I unconsciously "feel" is not pain; the screaming newborn does not feel pain. It certainly feels *something* and cries because it feels it, but that is not pain yet, indeed it has nothing negative yet: it can't have it because the newborn has no criterion or judgment of value available. Its crying is a simple physical reaction which *we* interpret as pain. Later, when society has "conditioned" it, that very crying *will become* an expression of pain—of a pain that does not belong to the foundations of subjectivity.

R: This is getting to be terribly confused. You said earlier that theorization originates from a crisis, and now you added that crisis and theorization constitute subjectivity. But a crisis would be a "figurative" example of pain, and pain would not belong to the foundations of subjectivity . . .

E: I too am having trouble here. On the one hand attention inaugurates transcendental language, and on the other it is supposed to be a secret service acting in the interest of the empirical world.

B: I realize now that I gave a hasty and unsatisfactory answer when Enrico brought out the ambiguity of the notion of a crisis. What we are talking about *is a crisis* only from the outside, because it's only from that point of view that it represents a problem. For the subject, the interruption of automatisms is a favorable opportunity, a power gap it can take advantage of in launching its transgressive activity . . .

E: . . . which in turn will be lived ideologically as an attempt to resolve the crisis.

B: Sure, and perhaps it will resolve it—in the sense we discussed, by reshuffling the deck. At any rate, my earlier response should be rephrased as follows: a certain species of individuals has this behavioral option available (among many), this capacity to utilize functional gaps as occasions for revolt—which is felt, by that consciousness which plays the existent's game, as the opening up of a crisis.

E: If you put it that way, on the other hand, the connection with the socio-political dimension becomes even clearer: the theoretical process will have to be controlled very closely.

B: It's no longer just a "connection," Enrico: the political dimension has become essential. We cannot limit ourselves to drawing the operational consequences of a metaphysical discourse: metaphysics itself is now deeply interwoven with power struggles and equilibria. Politics is now a metaphor that organizes everything we say.

E: So let's try to take this political discourse one step further. Let's admit, as you were saying before you were interrupted, that experience has a subject . . .

B: OK. In contrast with what happens in the realist paradigm, this will not at all entail the objectivity of the subject. It remains to be proved that the subject is an object, and to prove it one must coordinate the experiential perspectivism which gave the subject its original logical dignity with those characters of spatiotemporality—more precisely, of spatiotemporal continuity—which for an idealist are necessary conditions of existence.

E: But why should the subject become an object? Didn't we say that it *opposes* objects?

B: Sure, but if the opposition were radical, the otherness irreducible, the subject could not be a perspective on *this* reality, an agency trying to change it.

E: So the "channel" opened by consciousness—or personality—does serve both parties after all . . .

B: . . . and once again the image of the spy helps us get clearer. Think of how often foreign, even enemy, powers use their spies to establish contacts with one another. Unofficial contacts, of course, which can always be denied, and yet precious like no other. In the same way, the public world will exercise control on private transgression by infiltrating the subject with a personal, conscious structure to which (for good reason) one will end up attributing a foundational value for the subject itself (the mole is handier, the higher up it's placed), and at the same time the subject will use that structure to contaminate the environment with its subversion. If this kind of contamination were not possible, if the subject could not "come into the world," if there were not at least a theoretical capacity for communication, we could not speak of projects, of desires, or even of a criticism of what exists, but only of a madman preaching in the desert, or better still of an explosion occurring in a distant galaxy, under the protection of the cosmic void.

E: As in Epicurus's *intermundia* . . .

B: Well said, and it's more than a simple analogy. By emphasizing the public, communal features of objectivity, indeed making it coincide with those features, transcendental idealism naturally espouses a humanistic, antitheological project, where even the judgment passed on the world, to qualify as meaningful, must come to terms with that world, deal with it, translate itself into empirical, concrete recipes. The translation may always remain incomplete, unsatisfactory, and hence the subject may forever continue to posit itself as irremediably alien and critical, but without this persistent, uninterrupted effort, "criticism" would reduce to simple, trivial daydreaming.

E: Just as possibility would vanish in the nothingness of a set of random words if it did not accept the risk of putting forth at least a hypothesis of reality.

B: Right! And this analogy is not coincidental either, given the deep connection between subjectivity and the exploration of possibilities. Whereas, on the other hand, the realist's immediate, unquestioned ontological certainty lets him locate the subject at an infinite distance from the world *and rest content in this distance*, that is, treat the subject as an integral and self-sufficient god, as a unique and isolated being which constitutionally, by definition, cannot enter into a community.

E: So the philosophical drift must find some objective correlates.

B: The word "correlate" is exactly right. It's not by chance that this word is often used to indicate those courses-of-values which Frege associates with his concepts and which, as we already recalled, are the only things one can meaningfully talk about when one *tries* to talk about concepts. That's not by chance because the connection between a concept and its course-of-values is a very strict, I would almost say visceral, one. The course-of-values is not a simple, arbitrary representative of the concept in the realm of "saturated" entities, but rather is constituted by all and only the entities that satisfy the concept—the course-of-values of the concept *horse*, for example, is constituted by all and only the horses. Which means that there will be a precise, point-by-point correspondence between concept and course-of-values: every "mark" of the concept will be reflected by a property of the elements of the course-of-values. While it remains true that the most specific aspect of the concept—its unsaturated, indeed conceptual nature—must be lost in this operation, the connection thus established is certainly the strictest possible. In the same way, the subject will certainly lose its "subjectivity," its intrinsically elusive and rebellious character, when it agrees to come into the world, but aside from this feature no concessions will be made. It will not be enough to predicate an identity, to give the subject a body, to lodge it there as a pilot in a ship; it will be necessary to establish precise correspondences between the phenomenological characteristics of subjectivity (that is, the characteristics of that experience which has been assigned to the subject) and particular physical traits of the body. The subject's "point of view" will be reinterpreted as partiality of sensory access to the world, the incoherences and oddities of that point of view will be imputed to the periodical alternation of ordinary functionality and REM episodes, the resonance of experiences across time will be explained by the establishment of short- or long-term "traces," and so on. All this in the presence of a constant risk, unknown to the other paradigm: the risk that some such correspondences don't work, and that such a failure throws open a conceptual gap which swallows the subject's objectivity and eliminates it from the realm of existents, the risk that unpleasant empirical discoveries may deny to one of the physical properties used the presuppositions of that usage, and force us to look for something else that can take its place.

E: A risk which, if I understand you correctly, is analogous to the one knowledge faces in the realist paradigm.

B: Exactly. There it's knowledge that can "vanish" from one moment to the next, if for example a stick immersed in water looks broken, for then one will no longer know *what knowledge means*, hence will not know whether there is any. Here, on the other hand, the problem concerns objects, and the subject too *as an object*. Suppose for example that we identify the subject with the brain, and then one day we are able to successfully carry out a complete brain transplant. The most obvious prediction, on the basis of the identification we made, is that the subjectivity of the original carrier of the brain will get transferred into the new body. Can't you picture to yourself physicians, scientists, and philosophers as they anxiously wait for the patient to wake up, eager to know *who* will wake up? And suppose that the person who wakes up does not fit the prediction, that his memories, his intuitions, and his judgments are a strange mixture of those of the two previous people, or perhaps are entirely original. For the realist this result would certainly create problems, since for him too it is important to be able to recognize a subject empirically, but for the idealist the situation would be much more serious. For him at this point there would be no guarantee of the *existence* of a subject: a specific proposal attempting to provide this guarantee would have to be junked, and he would have to look for another one. Meanwhile, he would not know whether the subject exists because he would not know what it means for it to exist.

S: All this has a lot in common with what Enrico said earlier about needing to prove the consistency of an individual's intentional structure before we can ascribe a particular volitional episode to him.

E: Yes, but Angelo's position seems more radical. I limited myself to calling in question the adjective "my"—indeed, more precisely, certain uses of that adjective, since for example I spoke with no hesitation of *my* body. Whereas he calls in question the pronoun "I" to which the adjective refers: it's the pronoun that runs the risk of remaining empty.

B: Right, Enrico, and perhaps Angelo would see your remarks as a symptom that none of us is a pure example of one paradigm: we are all halfway, torn between opposite demands, trying various kinds of compromise.

Five

ROBERTO: I'm waiting for you to begin to speak about freedom. In all you've said so far, my purely factual language would work as smoothly as silk.

BERTOLDO: Perhaps, Roberto, but your language has limitations, which generate the *need*, not just the possibility or the convenience, to speak of actions, hence of free behavior.

ENRICO: The limitations represented by the antinomies, if I remember correctly.

B: Yes, and most specifically the second one. It is the indefinite divisibility of spacetime, and its destructive effect on the objectivity of what is located in spacetime, that force Angelo (and Kant before him) to understand experience in terms of a synthesis, hence as something that *is done*, not in a way determined by the structure of things but freely.

E: But this kind of talk seems a bit confused. Even if the antinomies proved that it's impossible to explain the positing of one object instead of another (for example, instead of the parts of the former) without admitting a more or less arbitrary "beginning" for this operation, and so forced us to include some form of freedom within the foundations of what exists, how does one go from *this* freedom to the notion of a synthesis, that is, of a free *act*? The arbitrary "freedom" we must accept could be pure and simple *chance*: a freedom without agents, like the electron's when it goes into a given eigenstate without having *decided* to do so (and without anyone deciding for it).

B: You're right, but it's not so much a confusion as an abbreviated train of reasoning, which lacks a few steps. At this point, however, we can probably supply the missing steps ourselves. I don't think that Angelo would pass a negative judgment on quantum physics, not on these grounds at least. But he would say that there is a substantial difference between the electron's behavior and the construction of the world—the *theoretical* construction of it, mind you . . .

E: Certainly the world is not to be "constructed" with hammer and nails.

B: In fact, we can imagine a situation in which the world is exactly the same but the choice we are talking about does not occur. In such a situation, we would continue to do the same things but we would not be able to *say* what it is that we do. We would use tables and chairs, but we could not call them that.

E: But calling them something is important too—practically, I mean.

B: Not directly, and not necessarily. Calling them something might get a process of drift and change started, but might also fizzle out as a simple epiphenomenon, a "purely intellectual" blind alley. At any rate, the difference with the electron's behavior is that the theoretical construction of the world is already conceived as carried out starting from *a subject's* experience. If we had ended up saying, "A table *is seen*," as you suggested earlier, we could admit that seeing a table (rather than, for example, an organized set of wood planks) is a random event, but if we say instead, "*I see* a table," then the selection of a level of reality expressed by this sentence belongs to someone, is situated within a precise perspective, identified with that perspective. And, after all, asserting that the subject chooses or synthesizes the world means nothing more than this: as the subject constitutes the world it at the same time constitutes *its own point of view* on the world and attributes that point of view *to itself*, that is, to that critical, reflective, and provocative agency to which it has assigned the same dignity as to the world. It means that the construction of the world is (once again) a political event: it does not hover in the quiet heaven of "disinterested" reflection but rather implies a claim, a conflict. It means that, within our form of life, *subjective* and *objective* are born together, as poles of an identical tension, as terms that recall and presuppose each other, and this polarity draws the essential contours of the map, of the conceptual grid by which we read experience, and provides the logical premises we utilize to understand what kinds of facts and things there can be. Space, for example, is not in the subject, or of the subject, because what is in space *is*, and the subject must be able to oppose everything that is, to deny it, to refute it. On the other hand, space is undifferentiated, and hence that differentiation which is necessary in order to constitute objects must originate elsewhere, outside space, outside everything that is, on a scene where it's possible to institute the confrontation between what is and what isn't, between real and fictitious matters, between the right reading and the wrong one. It's precisely this confrontation with nonbeing that being needs in order to be what it is, hence it is there that the choice founding its being must be located: where the confrontation takes place.

E: But, if that's all there is to it, what prevents me from understanding these repeated "acts of choice" as random events "happening" to the same subject? That they are "located" in the subject does not entail that they are *of* the subject.

B: You can put it that way if you want, but then the word "random" no longer makes much sense. Think of your experience as a story and ask yourself when an event in a story seems to occur at random: when it's strange, unexpected, when it's not "in character." But if such events occurred too often in the story that is your experience, little by little the experience would lose its unity, which for an idealist must be a structural one.

E: As in Kant's transcendental apperception.

B: That's right. A realist, who regards the subject as an object of a certain kind and experience as a property or state of that object, would have no difficulty conceiving the unity of even a very mixed-up kind of experience: it's the experience, he would say, of an insane subject, but it's still *one* because the subject that has it is one. For the idealist, however, who starts precisely with experience, or rather with *experiences*, it's not possible to stitch these experiences together in a unitary experience, in a single point of view, unless they manifest some continuity, some connectedness . . .

E: So, to summarize, when you describe the subject as active in the production of its experience, and not as a simple victim of chance . . .

B: . . . I'm predicating a structure for that experience, I'm saying that it's possible to find in it the traces of an organic position, of a unitary sense, of a coherent perspective which, while opposing the world, remains identical with itself, conforming to its own "law." And I am formulating, within a discourse whose political dimension I have already emphasized, a thesis which is indeed political, which belongs to the politics of experience: I'm saying that, for the alternative to being, to the confident and somewhat trivial repetitiveness of practices, really to have a dignity equal to that of being itself, this alternative too must posit itself, or rather must be posited, as a recognizable project, must avoid fragmenting in a thousand rivulets of unconnected and contradictory impulses.

E: But then activity is systematic passivity, freedom a chance without oddity . . .

B: Yes, and reason is organized madness. I don't think Angelo would rebel against "paradoxes" of this kind, nor should you, considering what you were saying earlier about the garage episode.

E: True: there is clearly an analogy between that example and the idealist framework . . .

R: Wait a minute: before you take off with this analogy of yours, let us ask ourselves whether we couldn't give a less sophisticated explanation for an object's "being there." I agree that space is undifferentiated, and that in principle there could be a table here or a set of wood planks or what have you. And we can admit, for the sake of discussion, that the subject is somehow involved in determining what there will be. But why should its role be that of choosing the level of reality, why should the identification of that level belong to it, express its point of view as opposed to what exists, and so on with the rest of that nonsense? Why shouldn't it rather express the conditioning the subject underwent, the fact that it's gotten used to seeing a table by an old habit, an established social practice? I assure you that, however hard I try, I can't see wood planks or molecules here, indeed I can't see anything other than a table. Talk about freely deciding to see it!

B: You're right, Roberto, but you were the first to distinguish between the empirical sense and the conceptual necessity (or possibility) of one's freedom, and to point out to Stefano that the two don't always go together. Here the situation is analogous. What you sketched may be excellent empirical psychology, and it may provide a brilliant explanation for my (empirical) conviction that I can (or cannot) do otherwise, whereas what we are talking about is a transcendental, logical requirement, which binds you even as you try to deny it. Even when you say, "I am conditioned," or, "I never choose anything," you are utilizing the very distinction between the I and the world, between subjective and objective, that we have been discussing. For all of us, including you, this distinction comes before any empirical discipline: without it one cannot even begin such a discipline. And notice that I'm not saying that things could not go differently, that it would not be possible for alien individuals to think and speak and live by other laws, or that you could not suddenly become an individual like that. I'm only saying that, if you did, we would probably no longer understand each other.

E: In what you say, on the other hand, there seems to be an implicit objection to the logical structure of the explanations current in quantum physics, which earlier you had cautiously decided to leave alone. If generalized, that logic would entail a loss of subjectivity, and hence of the critical, utopian function the subject fulfills in our form of life. It's not surprising that people of Einstein's caliber were dissatisfied with this kind of explanation.

B: Perhaps, Enrico, but I prefer to remain cautious. Even the evolution from dinosaurs to mammals has had as a consequence the loss of certain functions, or maybe just a different approach to the same functions, but such an outcome could not be the basis for an objection—since diversity is not automatically a *mistake*. Various signs today suggest that subjectivity as we understand it is becoming obsolete.

E: There are also those, of course, who without mincing words speak of the "death of the subject" . . .

B: . . . and often do so by way of inviting us to a worship of practice, of "writing," to a refusal of the mythopoetic force of the *logos*, to a meticulous, pedantic disclosing of the innumerable ideological facets of those myths—all of which fits perfectly the tendency to silence any alternative voice, any promise to attribute a "right" direction to history.

E: But how do you explain the fact that these ministers of the absurd, these executioners of the imaginary, construe themselves as performing a critical, destructuring, negative operation?

B: To answer that question we must return to politics as a metaphor, Enrico. You might unmask the Marxist dream by recalling Stalin's, Mao's, or Deng Xiaoping's massacres, and feel like a progressive because you are playing a demystifying role, but *if you do nothing else*—that is, if you don't substitute *another* myth, another hope for the Marxist one—you are in fact working to consolidate the existing structure, with all its injustices and horrors. Your refined analyses will in fact serve the interests of the rich and privileged, while in Soweto, in Dacca, and in Mexico City the damned of the earth will be left without a means to interpret themselves, to understand and articulate their rage and frustration.

E: So, in the same way, a criticism of every rational reconstruction that refuses to set itself up, in positive terms, as another rational reconstruction . . .

B: . . . that is, refuses to carry the burden of its own vanity . . .

E: . . . performs in fact the reactionary task of making every critical demand a dead letter.

B: Exactly: the ancient skeptics already realized that certain words have a destructive effect on every possible word, like a purge that, by emptying the intestine of all its contents, empties it also of itself. And we need not insist on the reactionary import of skepticism.

E: But you yourself refused to turn these considerations into objections, and spoke of dinosaurs and mammals and pure and simple diversity. Don't you think that the development we are talking about issues in a net loss for our species? If you are right, a "practice without theory" has become dominant in our attitude toward the physical world, and a "description without explanation" is acquiring more and more weight among our intellectuals.

B: Yes, sure, but we must avoid ethnocentrism and try to go beyond a simple defense of what there is, which incidentally would make us, despite our theoretical pretense, join those dreary characters you called "executioners of the imaginary." Perhaps what we are witnessing is not the disappearance of subjectivity; perhaps subjectivity is only moving.

E: What do you mean?

B: Remember when we spoke about computers, and about how dangerous it is to teach them to transgress orders? What worried us then, we can say now, was the risk of subjectivity, the risk that a computer might start making *its own* alternative proposals; but to be afraid of it and try to avoid it might not be enough. The most important things happen though no one wants them. So it might happen that, to make computers carry out our instructions more effectively, we get to the point of conferring on them a "critical" level of structural complexity, and at that point subjectivity, transgression, play *explode, emerge*. When a network begins to play it will no longer need subjects like us, and that moment may be close at hand: all the signs we have discussed, and many others we left aside, may be anticipations of it.

E: So the *Übermensch* might not be a creature in the flesh . . .

R: You are really priceless! You speak so much of explanations, of conceptual, mythical, narrative, or who knows what other tools to be offered to Soweto's wretches, bustle about casting shopworn doubts on the best physical *theory* available to us (instead of using it as an occasion for rethinking the very notion of a theory), even raise science-fictional ghosts to threaten our subjectivity, but what can *you* offer as an explanatory mechanism? How do *you* counter the nefarious "practice without theory"? What do you propose, other than the quick fix of calling "freedom" the *unexplainable* beginning of the causal chain? What is a reference to this freedom but an evocation of the ineffable, a labeling (and reifying) of shadows whose origin and structure you are the first to admit you know nothing about?

B: I could repeat that labeling and reifying those shadows is a much more complex operation than you imply: it's not just a matter of using words like "I," "choice," or "freedom" whenever we don't understand something, but also of aggregating such uses around a recognizable project, a coherent reform plan. And yet I don't want to deny that there is some sense in what you are saying: the need those words express does come from some other place, or indeed from no place at all because the existent world includes all places, and hence comes, can't but come, from the unknown, from what is constitutionally out of our reach, from something which we can, we must, continuously try to make comprehensible but which is also fated to remain, in its most intimate nature, *in*comprehensible. Despite all that, a reference to this need is not idle. Remember what we said about explanation: we try to understand something better but meanwhile we shift farther and farther away, and if at some point we really understand—that is, we stop searching—it's only because the process as a whole has worked as an unconscious Pygmalion for different and more effective practical moves. You are entirely sold on the foundational ideology: for you to speak of freedom, of a starting point, means to refuse to dig deeper into the essence of phenomena. For Angelo, however, it means only to interrupt for a moment the reality of the scattering which is hidden under that ideology, to acknowledge the "transcendental illusion" animating this circuitous journey . . .

E: Without denying its necessity.

B: Exactly: the illusion is an indispensable component of our overall balance, and ruling it out would mean going to work for a different "master." But it's useful, once in a while, to critically emphasize its delusional character, and to return to conceiving the phenomenon—any phenomenon—in all of its mystery: an unknowable and unexplainable entity not because *it* is anything special or defective but because the very project of explaining has inevitably dialectical outcomes.

R: It has such outcomes for you, because you can't mediate between facts and your unsatisfiable demands. What's wrong with an explanatory process that takes us always farther and never comes to an end, but meanwhile reveals ever more concealed connections among the various aspects of reality? Aren't you, who accuse me of foundationalism, getting off a bit cheaply by interrupting this process with a simple short circuit: the world begins here, where *I want* it to begin?

B: It's not that simple, Roberto, and perhaps it's not Angelo who gets off cheaply. The "unsatisfiable demands" you're talking about are tensions which organize experience, and which it's impossible to leave aside without transforming experience into something else—something possibly easier to conceptualize but harder to recognize as our own. And you have your unsatisfiable demands too: your desire for explanation is one of them, and to speak of it as something that gets satisfied through an infinite sequence of steps is nothing but a way of labeling your problem, to use your own terms. You are very sensitive to the vacuity of our reference to a free beginning, to its nature as a "short circuit," but do you think you are better off when instead of saying, "there will never be an explanation," you incorporate the negation into the predicate (thus constituting what Kant would have called, not accidentally, an *infinite* judgment) and say, "explanation is an interminable process"?

R: But these are reactionary objections. From Cantor on, the analysis of the concept of infinity has gone well beyond the "negative theology" you attribute to me. There is now a whole branch of mathematics that shows how to manipulate countable and uncountable sets, how to assert or deny properties and relations of them, how to add them up and multiply them.

B: To tell you the truth—and to be reactionary all the way, if you will—your "mathematics of infinity" shows only how to manipulate some strange symbols, *all rigorously finite*. Then there is also the claim that the symbols refer to countable or uncountable sets, and that by manipulating the symbols one describes appropriate manipulations of those sets, but given that it's impossible to prove the consistency—that is, the reliability—of all this machinery, one must be very sympathetic in order to take the claim seriously. Whoever is not that sympathetic will find a reference to infinity as mysterious as a reference to freedom, and will consider favoring the one just as arbitrary as favoring the other. Whereas by admitting them both we will be able to attain a more credible conception of experience: neither the abstract scientism you like to masquerade in nor the trivial voluntarism you are trying to get me stuck with, but a continuous oscillation, a continuous conflict of functions. "Someone" must have established a language to speak the world, must have chosen this language among all theoretically possible ones. There is a subject for this story, a narrator, but who is it? Is it this body, some part of it, some mechanism lodged in it, or is it something larger: a society, a tradition, a class, a people? Or, again, is language itself perhaps the true subject, the only agent; is it language that speaks us all? Someone—or something—must be free: this is as valid a transcendental requirement as the one for explanation, and it's just as difficult to coordinate it with empirical realities, to "realize" it by a projection into that spatiotemporal world where existence "takes place."

STEFANO: But this freedom of yours seems quite strange: it's a theoretical freedom to describe the world as we like, rather than the practical freedom that I talk about—the freedom to perform actions, to take responsibility and possibly the blame for them.

E: Yes, and there is also something else. Usually we speak of freedom as concerning the future. I believe I'm free because I believe that I can choose now what I will do tomorrow, or in a minute, or an hour. Whereas your freedom seems to concern the past: in order to explain the fact that experience is determinate, that it is this experience rather than any other, I must postulate *as having already occurred* some acts of free choice on the part of someone, and then possibly go in search of who that someone was. How then shall we deal—how would Angelo deal—with the projectional, appetitive nature of action, that is, of free behavior, of willed behavior? Action does not retrospectively reconstruct the world but changes it, makes the world that comes *after* different from the one that was *before*.

R: My demand might be unsatisfiable too, Bertoldo, but at least it's clear. You guys, on the other hand, who feel the need to speak of freedom, are not even sure you all speak about the same thing.

B: That might not be so strange, Roberto. Perhaps all we can do is use *the same word*, facing the risk of its ambiguity, asking ourselves courageously under what conditions it would be legitimate to deny that ambiguity . . .

E: . . . and giving up the facile reassurance of mutual understanding provided by the realist paradigm.

B: Well said, Enrico! For those who start with things it is natural to assume from the beginning (and without further discussion) an identity of objectual reference, whereas for those who must arrive at things this identity is a problem . . .

E: . . . around which seems to surface again, and to get clearer, that debate of yours about dogs and legs: whether, that is, language has an essential role in the determination of what exists.

B: True. For the realist the world does not depend conceptually on language, so it's possible to conceive its structure without bringing in the notion of a language; for the idealist on the other hand . . .

S: Enough with metaphilosophical talk! Freedom, then . . .

Six

BERTOLDO: The fact is that metaphilosophical talk comes easier; when we get to specifics, Angelo's statements are difficult to articulate in a comprehensible manner. These two problems you raised, for example . . . indeed, maybe, *this one* problem, for I think that the problem for him would always be the same . . .

ENRICO: You mean that freedom to act and freedom in the future coincide?

B: Probably Angelo would say that the future is a necessary dimension of an action, a conceptual requirement for it, that in order to speak of something as an action we must be able to speak of a future *it* has, and hence refer to the future, to the idea of the future . . .

E: Even if the action is past . . .

B: Exactly: even if it happened yesterday, or last year, or at the beginning of the world. To interpret it as an action, rather than a simple sequence of movements, means to project an intentionality on it, a plan . . .

ROBERTO: But he's opposed to intentions!

B: He's opposed to intentions as an explanatory mechanism, as a ghost in the machine that accounts for its workings, not as *an issue to be addressed*. It is an undeniable fact that we attribute intentions to others

57

and to ourselves; we need to understand what that attribution means, what it comes down to.

E: A reference to the future?

B: I'd say, yes. To attribute to someone the "intention" of drinking means to create expectations about the evolution of his behavior, and to read certain movements of his as actions directed to the realization of that intention means to frame them within the expectations thus formed—expectations concerning something that is not yet, something future.

E: In short, to use the terminology so dear to Angelo, if in a logical space there were no future there couldn't be actions either.

B: Yes, and this may be why we find it natural—phenomenologically, that is, in terms of our *hic et nunc*—to locate that freedom which is an essential feature of actions, which distinguishes them from pure and simple behavior, in the future of our *hic et nunc*, in what is properly called future, not in what was once future but is no longer that.

E: For there we find an immediate correspondence between the conceptual requirement and the empirical datum, and we can make immediate use of the latter to satisfy the former.

STEFANO: Before you get too satisfied I would like to remind you that so far you have only reduced the number of problems, but did not resolve them. We still need to relate this freedom to act in the future with the freedom to interpret one's past, which if I am not mistaken we were left with.

B: You're right, but here I would have a hard time saying anything definite. I can give you formulas that sound subtle and deep, as long as you don't ask me what they mean. For example, Angelo often says that reading, interpreting, is the only true action, the primordial one.

S: But that is a joke! Clearly, if we accepted it then everything would be resolved, and the freedom to act would become a purely hermeneutic matter, but why should we accept it? Reading is the opposite of acting: it's ceasing to plan the future and limiting oneself to receiving the past.

E: Perhaps it's all less absurd than you think, Stefano. A certain form of reasoning has emerged more than once in our discussion and seems central in Angelo's philosophical practice. Bertoldo said—remember?— that in a world of facts there are no facts, and then that experience comes into being only when one questions it, and then again that it's we who interpret what the newborn feels as pain. In all these cases the general sense was the same: there are structures that can be perceived only from some *other* point of view, only when something *else* is called in and used as a term of reference. A fact *becomes* a fact when we project a theory, an explanation, onto it; a pure fact is not even a fact, is not *yet* a fact. Analogously, what is done would not be an action yet if it were not inserted in a line of thought that essentially includes the future—that is, something that goes beyond the action itself, that does not belong to it but nonetheless makes it an action. But now let us ask ourselves: Where is this future? Where shall we find it? Is the future part of the world, part of the facts? Clearly not. The present is part of the world, and maybe the past too if we agree that a sufficient condition for *being* is being somehow *determined*, being thus and so and not otherwise.

R: But the future is determined too! It's absolutely determined *now* whether it will rain tomorrow, and whoever believes it's not is just confusing metaphysics with epistemology, the reality of facts with our limited capacity to predict them.

E: It's always the same thing, Roberto: you just can't see any alternative to your realist notion of truth, even despite the fact that in this case there are some prize realists who took positions subtler than yours. Aristotle, to mention one of them, in the *De Interpretatione* has an at least unsettled attitude on the determinacy of a sentence like, "There will be a sea-battle tomorrow."

R: Look, quotes do not impress me. I have no difficulty admitting that Aristotle could be confused!

E: Your independence of judgment is laudable, but why don't you try thinking that what you describe a bit hastily as "confusion" might just be a different *definition* of truth . . .

B: Better yet: a different order of definitional priority.

E: Right, for we may never get to a definition, we may never be able to, but certainly an idealist will *look for* it by considering the ways experiences structure and articulate themselves, so the absence of relevant experiences in the case of the sea-battle tomorrow will have decisive weight for his *metaphysical* conclusions on that question.

R: But then relevant experiences are lacking for the past too, and hence the past too "does not exist"! So what *does* exist: only the fleeting moment?

E: No, because the experiences we lack concerning the past we lack because of practical limitations, whereas here we are talking at a theoretical, conceptual level, in terms of logical, not empirical accessibility.

R: So far I've heard very little that is theoretical—by which I mean, rationally argued. I've heard a lot that is "narrative," however: gratuitous assumptions, groundless pronouncements . . .

E: I will try to oblige you. So the future does not exist: it's what could be, and perhaps will be, but is not yet. Then what is it to refer to it, to make it an object of discourse? Doesn't this discourse get annihilated, lose all its content? At the stage we have reached, these questions are not hard to answer: in order to avoid the emptiness that threatens it, a reference to the future must be understood as a reference to the projectional character of our being in the world, to our seeing the world in the light of a plan—a plan which is projected onto the world to make sense of our movements, of our behavior. *Sense*, you understand, *meaning*: without meaning there is no future. Without a meaningful story, an explanation, a tale that calls it in question and suddenly reveals it as a pervasive, authoritarian presence, capable of assigning a place and a value to all that precedes it, the future would be nothing but a black hole, a nonentity, a zombie to revive by transfusing it with our own blood, the blood of us who are the only ones *being*—being *now*, which is the only way to be.

B: The "transfusion" you are talking about seems to describe Roberto's determinism perfectly.

E: That's right: for a determinist the future has nothing new to say, it's already written in what has already happened. Its being is parasitic, dependent, anaclitic. What will happen is the object of a derivation, not of a discovery, and can surprise us only because we are dominated by laziness and ignorance. It's certainly not on a future like that that we can found a discourse of freedom: we need something more vital, richer, something that can speak with its own voice.

B: To summarize, then, the future is a conceptual condition of an action, meaning is a conceptual condition of the future . . .

E: . . . and the practice that presents itself as constitutive of meaning, which makes it be—the practice of reading, explaining, interpreting—is a conceptual condition of meaning, of the future, and of an action. It is itself an action, mind you: the second antinomy has proved that it couldn't be otherwise, that without postulating an absolute beginning, a free choice, it would be impossible to account for the fact that we read in one way and not another. But it's also the primordial, original action: the one we must refer to, more or less explicitly, to be able to speak of any action at all.

B: An outcome as inevitable as it is paradoxical: that very interpretive practice of which philosophy is the purest expression and which earlier, because of its experimental, playful nature, we described as essentially *in*active, now comes to be the logical foundation of every activity, that is, of all those things which, insofar as they are repetitive, coherent, recognizable, it is legitimate to regard as specific activities. One could say that the *phenomenon* of action rests on an incomprehensible and unknowable conceptual need, on a transcendental, noumenal freedom, logically necessary and at the same time rigidly excluded from experience, ineluctably distant from the solid habits in which our life and our reality manifest themselves.

E: Just as, on the other hand, and according to what we have already seen, every phenomenal object "rests," depends for its being, for its nature, for its very having a nature, on an object—or rather subject—"of thought" which as such *is not*, is foreign to the world.

S: Wait a minute, I'm lost: so there will be freedom only in the past, only in reading?

E: No, Stefano, you will be free, you will judge empirically (and correctly, in the only sense in which we can speak of correctness—the empirical, practical one) that you are free as much in the future as in the past. But suppose now that someone asks for an explanation of this judgment of yours, that he asks a why question about it. Well, our bet—or rather, Angelo's—is that, eventually, your answer will have to appeal to the activity of interpretation, of the world and of yourself. For example, you might say: "I freely choose to quit this discussion and go home to study." And I might ask you what authorizes you to say that, what makes you think that you are not rather the object of a subtle form of conditioning, and you might answer: "The fact that studying falls within my plans, agrees with my constant desire to be successful in my career, whereas staying here longer would be deeply uncharacteristic of me." And again I could ask you why, and you would cite me all sorts of evidence that you are really like that, that that's really your character, that if anything any form of conditioning would distract you from your study, not invite you to it. And then it would be easy to point out that to justify your assertion of freedom you are interpreting your past, and that without this possibility of interpretation there would be no room to speak defensibly of an action that is truly yours, that truly belongs to you.

B: It's interesting to compare what you are saying now—and indeed had already emerged in our discussion—with the two classical conceptualizations of freedom cited earlier by Roberto: freedom as being able to do something other than what one does, or on the other hand as being able to do what one does independently of external influences. In Angelo's framework it's always the second notion that comes to light.

E: And are you surprised? It was you who emphasized the risk always present in the idealist paradigm: that of losing the subject, of seeing it

swallowed in its "objective" individuality by a universe not just epistem-
ically confused (the worst that could happen to the realist) but ontologi-
cally competitive. For those who don't confront that risk, proving one's
freedom will often mean insisting on the most arbitrary, odd, unrepeat-
able aspects of one's behavior . . .

B: Or the most absurd ones. The kind of unmotivated, repulsive
cruelty displayed by the "monster" responsible for these crimes is sometimes regarded as a supreme example of freedom: a Promethean, impu-
dent declaration that we need no rules, we are tied to no patterns.

E: Yes, and Angelo would probably view these outcomes with sympathy, and consider them the foundation of a reductio argument in favor of
his position. For him, at any rate, and in general for the idealist, the situation must be different: as with Kant, freedom will primarily mean
auto*nomy*, that is, it will be conceived as the expression of a *law*, self-
imposed and intrinsic to be sure but still a law. So one will have to find
this law, and prove the identity of the subject with itself, its recogniz-
ability in the most disparate contexts, as provided with a certain level of
resistance to those contexts, a certain capacity to move in them without
giving rise to *a*nomic, unreasonable manifestations.

B: One could even say: provided with a certain *degree* of freedom.

E: Exactly. In this picture, freedom is not a global, all-or-nothing attribute, but a project to be developed moment by moment, occasion by
occasion. Earlier I was interrupted while I tried to focus on the affinity
between the idealist paradigm and the garage episode; now I may be able
to explain what I had in mind. It will indeed be by putting (or imagin-
ing) myself in "deviant" situations like that, and more generally in envi-
ronments different from the theater of my everyday rituals, those
centered around my family, my work, and my "entertainment"; and,
progressing further in this deviance, by putting myself in climates and
places and cultures which are entirely foreign to me—this will be how I
painstakingly attempt to establish (without ever finally succeeding) that
I cannot be reduced to an efficient little wheel in the mechanism of my
habits, my place, and my culture, that I can continue to turn more or less
at the same velocity and in the same direction even if the connections
with that mechanism are loosened, even if the current is cut off.

B: Whereas for the realist . . .

E: For the realist, as you yourself noticed, the subject is *already* an object, the I is what it is and does what it does. So one can speak straight-
forwardly of what the subject—*that very* subject, that very object which
is the subject—would do in another situation, and define freedom by an

essential reference to such alternative realities: the I is free because it could do otherwise, that is, because in other possible situations it would do otherwise. For the idealist, however, the discourse of alternatives must be legitimized in every single case: to be able to say what the subject would do in different circumstances we must first *find* it in those circumstances, identify it, distinguish it . . .

B: . . . which suggests a reflection of a formal character. As you know, there are two fundamental conceptions of a possible situation—or "world." According to the first one, which might be called combinatorial and goes back at least to Wittgenstein, another possible world is another possible way in which *these* things could have gone, all and only the things that exist *here*, in *this* world. According to the second one instead, which might be called descriptive and should perhaps be associated with Hilbert's formalist school and the development of model theory, a possible world is a structure that can be described in the language, a "model" of the language. The two conceptions must face different problems; specifically, the descriptive conception must face the problem of establishing whether, and under what conditions, an object in a world can be regarded as identical with an object in another world—a problem which the combinatorial conception avoids, rather than resolving, by introducing a demonstrative element right at the beginning and using it to "fix" references. What you are saying now suggests that a similar problem of "identification through possible worlds" exists for transcendental idealism too, hence that the descriptive conception is the one closer to this philosophical position, just as the combinatorial conception probably agrees more with realism . . .

E: . . . which is not strange when you consider that the two conceptions go in opposite directions, respectively identical with the directions of realism and idealism: the combinatorial one goes from the world to language, and the descriptive one from language to the world. When Kant says that nature for him is not a set of objects but a set of laws, he's emphasizing precisely this change of perspective: while it remains true that there are *both* objects *and* laws in the world, it's laws that make objects possible, not vice versa. That is, it's through the establishing of a system of nomic, rational regularities that one can substantiate the existence of a set of beings, and even their "continuing to be" in different situations (for example, in time), not rather (as happened traditionally) through a reference to the definiteness of those beings that one can justify their rationality, and hence their intelligibility, and hence the possibility of subsuming them under a system of laws. It is the laws that *make* the world, that is, that turn the object (the intentional, not yet real object, hence properly speaking one that is not yet an object) of our experience into *a world*, and not rather the world that makes the laws . . .

B: . . . and this attitude will have a profound effect on the very notion of a law. Think of the authors (Kelsen, say) who asserted the conceptual priority of laws in the legal sense with respect to laws in the scientific sense—the "laws of nature" you were talking about. The way they often put it, man regulates his own behavior by imposing precise limitations and duties on himself and his fellow humans *and then*, anthropomorphizing with a vengeance, ends up imposing rules on what is not human too. This scheme may seem obvious to the realist, who does not problematize the identity of objects and hence that of the subject either, but for the idealist things must be just the other way around: it is only by adopting toward himself the observational attitude he's already applied to nature—better, the attitude that let him constitute a "nature" in the first place—in short it's by discovering regularities in his actions, identifying their laws, that man can make a subject surface, and around it aggregate a community and a sense of legality.

E: Which, if you think about it, is one more example of those curious and suggestive paradoxes Angelo's position is studded with . . .

B: . . . and that are paradoxes only because our language is not adequate to it.

E: Perhaps. What I mean is that the necessity expressed by the laws of nature is considered the exact opposite of freedom. We ourselves have used this contrast: it's the intrinsic limitations of natural explanation, we said, that force us to posit a free, primordial act of choice. But when we articulated this point and gave more detail on what is meant by freedom, we were led to attribute to the subject—to what *is* free, that is—a necessity at least analogous to that of natural laws.

B: This reminds me that the authors who are inclined to understand freedom as autonomy—one name among many: Spinoza—are also inclined to insist on a coincidence between freedom and necessity.

E: True, and that view always sounds mysterious and a bit strained, as if one wanted to make things add up at all costs, to save both responsibility and predestination, and who knows what other theological dogma. Whereas theology does not even come into it, not necessarily at least . . .

B: In fact, it's the humanization of these themes, that public, communitarian view I mentioned earlier, which brings about the identification.

E: Right! When one says that authentic freedom consists of accepting necessary laws, one is not vainly chattering about a mystic *coincidentia oppositorum*: one is rather following a rigorous logical process to its ultimate consequences. We brought up this point a while ago, and now we can confirm it and make it more precise: the subject is something more than a grammatical fiction or a need for transgression, it *is*, in short, *really* is—and hence is also free—only when its cipher appears with implacable consistency, when its specificity weaves an uninterrupted texture, its essence abolishes fortuitous events and necessarily determines every element of that experience which only thus can legitimately be called *its own*.

S: Which means that I, for one, am not a subject, since I can't possibly attribute to myself such implacable consistency.

E: You're right, Stefano: to be a subject in this perspective is not something that can be taken for granted. It's rather a delicate, complex, and probably endless task. One is not born a subject and does not suddenly become one—not, at least, in *objective* terms. One must rather painstakingly search for one's individuality, overcome all accidental and extrinsic determinations . . .

S: Pardon my interruption, but I can't see my way in all of this. You keep referring to the *concept* of freedom, to freedom as a rational construct, or to the logical consequences of a *discourse* on freedom, but I think of how I *feel* free, how I'm convinced that, if I want, I can say, "The hell with you." Is there room in your scheme of things for *this* freedom, which is the only one I care about?

Seven

BERTOLDO: We are back at square one, Stefano: at the correspondence between empirical data and conceptual requirements. Your "feeling" is a datum, and as such is intrinsically ambiguous. You consider it an expression of freedom, but what could you object if you were told instead that it's simply the result of a tension between the indeterminacy of your future behavior, which cannot be known since it does not yet exist, and the need, I'd say the biological need, on the part of an organism like yours, to assert some form of control on that behavior, to appropriate it, through a programmatic (but vain) "declaration of intent"? To read this datum in terms of freedom means to use it to provide some concreteness for an abstract concept, a concept whose necessity is established at a theoretical level, by a rational argument. Such an argument on the other hand—Angelo says, and this seems to me the most brilliant intuition of his metaphilosophy— does not settle all accounts, does not seal the issue, but rather proposes the endless task of making that concept concrete, of instantiating it.

STEFANO: I continue to be mystified. Even if I failed in this task and never discovered the "uninterrupted texture" of my life, I wouldn't for that reason stop feeling myself, or feeling free.

ENRICO: You don't have to discover it: you must *think* that it can be discovered.

B: Exactly. Discovering it is an empirical fact; or rather, it would be an empirical fact if it happened. Whereas what we are talking about is a logical possibility.

S: I insist that your scheme is too intellectualistic. The possibility you are talking about never comes to mind, has no role in my life: at most I think of it when I'm doing philosophy. And yet . . .

B: . . . you feel something, and call that feeling free, or feeling yourself. About the feeling as such we have nothing to say, but we do have something to say about what it's called: our thesis is located at that semantic level. You might never worry about straightening up your story, never think that that's important, but if you were not (at least obscurely) convinced that you could do it (if you felt the need), you might perhaps still feel what you feel but it would not be legitimate for you to call it what you call it.

E: And in fact this obscure conviction would become conscious if we asked you (as we imagined earlier) to account for your use of the word "free," to justify it.

ROBERTO: But then freedom is an illusion, idle talk! I find it convenient to think that I'm free, to be convinced of that; as for really being it . . .

B: Angelo could even accept that, but he would make at least two objections. First, freedom is no more idle talk than facts are: both facts and freedom exist, are constituted at the level of idle talk, of theory, of chattering about experience—an experience that has already taken place. Second, this entails no negative judgment on freedom or on facts. There exists a practice of chattering to which we have assigned (by chattering) purposes as important as to the practices of (say) eating and mating, and calling it delusive means at most that, to perform its tasks better, this practice must be lived subjectively with a certain amount of bad faith, of false consciousness, must present itself as something else, as "nobler" and more (immediately) profitable than it is.

R: But these conclusions clash with the Kantian framework within which you keep setting Angelo's views. As far as I know, Kant emphasizes the guiding role of ideas and plans, their regulative function—whether or not it's possible to realize them empirically—and hence would not agree to reduce them to retrospective justifications, to pious but vain words of reassurance. The image one draws from reading Kant is that of an agent who is moved by his perception of a goal, who desires to reach that goal, and behaves as if he could reach it. Then perhaps the goal turns out to be fictitious, the focus to which our efforts are directed

proves imaginary, and going toward it we obtain results that are foreign
or even opposite to our expectations, but it remains true that those expectations *moved us*, hence that they come *before* our moving, and cannot
be exiled to a purely rational, a posteriori reconstruction of experience.

E: I knew that sooner or later we would have to return to desire.

B: And you were right, Enrico, because it's precisely over desire that
idealists and realists fight their bloodiest and most delicate battle. This is
the key to their confrontation, and it's here that we must look if we want
to resolve Roberto's perplexities once and for all.

E: I suspected that much, but I would like to know the details.

B: Let's take a step backwards, in terms of the Kantian corpus; that is,
let's go from the second (or, if you will, the third) *Critique*, where the
concept of desire is central, to the first one, where what is central is the
concept of knowledge. If we compare these works, we notice something
strange: one of them is much *longer* than the other one (indeed, than
both of the others). And we might ask why.

E: Because the subject matter is more complex.

B: Perhaps, but this is not enough of an answer yet: for, at first sight,
it would seem that moral philosophy has at least as much conceptual
depth and richness as epistemology. So a new question arises: why is the
latter so much more complex *from the Kantian point of view*?

R: Maybe in the first *Critique* Kant is simply more confused, has more
trouble articulating his perspective, and hence the exposition is more
cumbersome and wordy.

B: It's a reasonable hypothesis, though some parts of the other *Cri-
tiques* rival anything Our Author has written in obscurity and convolut-
edness. At any rate, there is an alternative hypothesis, which is worth
bringing out: that Kant has unfortunately chosen to start from what, in
his new and revolutionary conceptual scheme, had to be the hardest
case.

E: So the first *Critique* should have been the last one?

B: That's right, but let's not get ahead of ourselves. Transcendental
idealism, we know, goes from ideas (experiences, representations) to objects, and transcendental realism goes in the opposite direction. So one
might ask in which direction our "empirical" life goes, that experience
of ours which idealism and realism are supposed to theorize about, to
conceptualize, and a first, rather plausible answer to this question is that
life does not always go in the same direction: experiences are not homo-
geneous in this respect. If I see a table, that will be lived empirically as
an adjustment of my perceptual structure to the existence and proper-

ties of the table, that is, as a result of an influence that the table, the *ob-ject* table, has on my capacity for representation: in this case, therefore, the direction is from the object to the idea. But if I look for a unicorn, or the phoenix, or the philosophers' stone, that will be lived as an attempt to adjust the world to a representation of mine, to make it fit a require-ment which started out as purely ideal: here the direction is from the idea to the object. In short, there is a deep affinity between idealism and appetitive experiences on the one hand, and realism and cognitive expe-riences on the other. And this affinity, or rather this *lack* of affinity be-tween the general Kantian program and the phenomenological structure of knowledge, this sharp "ideological" dissonance between the task to be performed and the tool to be used, explains the dreadful conceptual complications of the first *Critique*.

E: Including the fact, if I remember correctly, that realism must be called in question for the sake of articulating idealism.

B: Precisely. To account for knowledge within the idealist scheme one cannot avoid an instrumental use of the opposite scheme, and hence a painstaking translation of the latter's conditions within the former. All of this for a very simple reason: because knowledge inevitably recalls a realist style of thinking.

E: So realists should have similar problems with desire.

B: And indeed they do. To this day, realists have not been able to give us even an inkling of a logic of desire, that is, to suggest how to think of it and reason about it. In the last few decades there has been a multipli-cation of logics of all kinds: deontic and epistemic, causal and temporal. But we don't hear any talk of an optative logic, and that's because con-temporary logic has a realist framework, based on the notion of an object and hence irremediably foreign to volitional experiences. Every formal semantics—that is, every rigorous explanation of the meaning of a lan-guage—starts by postulating one or more domains, that is, by announc-ing: "Let there be a set (or several sets) *of objects*." Given that starting point, the semantics can account for almost anything: truth and validity, necessity and essence, probability and moral obligation. But the starting point itself cannot be explained, and that starting point is what makes a theorization of desire problematic.

E: Not only of desire: nondenoting singular terms too . . .

B: Yes: for those who start with objects it's natural to see names as properties of the objects named, and hence a name that names nothing becomes an absurdity, with obvious complications for the project of freeing logic from ontology and speaking also of what does not exist—or maybe of what we are not yet sure exists, of what we are trying to prove exists (think of the ontological argument for the existence of God again, and of how difficult it is to even phrase it in "classical" formal logic).

E: These complications and difficulties, in fact, are not unrelated to the previous ones: many of those who try the "liberation" you are talking about define singular terms as the expressions which *purport*—one might almost say, "desire"—to denote an object.

B: Thus reducing to a simple terminological assimilation the much deeper analogy between an experience that makes ideas prior to the world and a language that makes its own structures (for example, in the case of singular terms, the position of logical subject) prior to the structures of reality. But let's stay with desire, and consider once more the situation in which I am looking for a unicorn. Of course, there is no need that a unicorn exist for my experience to be what it is and have the structure it has: even if there were no unicorns (as in fact is the case), that would still be the experience of looking for a unicorn and not for example a donkey, or nothing. Now suppose I find a unicorn, that is, I have a perception, which I judge to be veridical, of an animal that corresponds exactly to my idea of a unicorn: clearly, at that point my experience of looking for a unicorn would immediately *terminate*. So there are cases—not all cases, to be sure, for I can also look for something I know exists, as when I look for my pen or my wallet . . .

E: But even then you don't know that they still exist, that they have not been destroyed.

B: Right: the point may be more general than I thought. There are cases anyway in which an appetitive experience is incompatible with the other experiences that would sanction the existence of its object. So if we try to account for this experience in terms of that reality which is the realist's conceptual foundation we come to a dead end: as soon as reality enters the picture, the experience we were interested in dissolves.

E: You mean, "as soon as *the experience* of reality enters the picture."

B: But that's exactly the problem, because we are trying to characterize an experience. Suppose that the experience of looking for a unicorn does not cease when one finds it—or rather, when one has the experience of finding it—or that the experience of wanting a child does not cease when one perceives its birth. Then one might be able to explain what experience it is—and more generally *what it is*—to look for a unicorn or to want a child by referring to the unicorn one has in fact found or the child one has in fact had, and then extend that explanation to the previous state (which in this case would be *the same* state). As things are, however, such a reference is impossible: it's only the *desired* child (or unicorn) that enters an experience of desire, not the real one, and hence the real one is of no use.

E: Perhaps it is of no direct use. One might be able to use it some other way.

B: That can't be denied. But the ways it's been used so far have always generated additional problems. It has been claimed, for example, that desiring is nothing but regretting a lost state—the Garden of Eden or the world of ideas or prenatal bliss—but clearly the experience of regretting a lost parent is very different, is lived very differently, from that of desiring a child not yet born, and it's only by assuming very bold metaphysical hypotheses (concerning for example some previous life of ours and our partial forgetfulness of it) that the analogy can be sustained.

E: Apropos of analogies, there seems to be a strict one between desire and philosophy. Just as the former has room only for the object *qua* desired, and hence *qua* purely intentional, the latter (as we have seen) is constitutionally incapable of getting integrated into the world, of becoming a real practice.

B: Sure, but it's an analogy present in *this* philosophy, in idealism. For here desire is the paradigmatic case, rational requirements come first, and the problem is how "reason can be practical," that is, how the desire expressed by those requirements can be fulfilled. If it cannot be fulfilled, one might say (and Kant sometimes does say), so much the worse for practices and for the world. Within realism on the other hand, where the paradigmatic case is knowledge, even philosophy presents itself as adjusting to a preconstituted reality, to the conceptual universe Roberto was talking about earlier . . .

S: Or to Frege's third *Reich*, the "empire of the senses" . . .

R: . . . and thus we are back at Hitler.

E: Leaving aside folkloristic excesses, I would like to recapitulate the difficulties realists have with desire. For this purpose consider again a distinction we used when we discussed the "crisis" from which theories originate. Either realists give an "internal" characterization of desire, and then they must face the conflict between the experience of desire and the experience (which for them must be foundational) of ascertaining the existence of the desired object, or they give an "external" characterization of it, and then they are locked into a dilemma: they can either violate the phenomenological structure of desire (brutally reducing this experience to something else) or, in order not to violate it (that is, in order to make their reduction credible), accept unwarranted hypotheses about what is external, about the world.

B: Well said! With respect to desire, realism has proved impotent.

R: But this only shows I'm right! In Kant, then, we don't find the conceptual "starting point" that creates all these complications for the realist: the desire that projects, prefigures reality, and directs our behavior is the primary sort of experience. So how can a Kantian claim that plans and projects are a posteriori rationalizations?

E: Yes; I'm missing the general sense of what you're saying, too.

B: That's because you are not making full use of the affinity we brought out between idealism and desire. That is, you're not using it to see what idealism—as a philosophical position—can tell us about desire.

E: I don't understand you.

B: A little earlier I asked myself in which direction our empirical life goes, and gave "a first answer" which I judged "rather plausible" . . .

E: You mean to say now that that answer was false?

B: No; I mean to say that the question was not a good one. Empirical life doesn't go in any direction, we know already, we spoke about it when we discussed the hypothesis of a purely practical existence, and between idealism and desire there is more than an affinity: there is a continuity of attitude. Both situate themselves in the context of that confabulation on experience which, insofar as it posits experience as an object of discourse, must be posterior to it, at least logically. Part of this confabulation is aimed at decisive moments of check and inquiry, and is thus immediately recognizable; some other part accompanies experience as a soft buzz, resolving small crises and tiny disturbances without getting noticed, appeasing internal tensions and conflicts, reassuring us of the consistency of our moves . . .

E: . . . and ruling out the possibility of a "purely practical" experience.

B: Better: showing "purely practical experience" to be a theoretical construct, a residue of a logical analysis of real experience. At any rate, confabulation will do all of this, in both the more conspicuous and the more homely cases, by using at least two tools, two narrative techniques: one in terms of efficient and one in terms of final causes. The former will tend to reassure us by inserting events into a large, complex mechanism, the latter by interpreting them as expressions of our own or someone else's intentions; both will move within the scope of that performance which in the most serious cases takes up the whole burden of the situation, replaces ordinary action entirely, and makes us, rather

than live, speculate on the ways in which what happens is the fruit, alternatively, of either a causal chain or a plan.

E: So what do all the references to regulative ideas and imaginary foci
. reduce to?

B: To the contrast between theory and practice—between facts and
"idle talk," to use Roberto's phrase. The notion of desire works as much
(or as little) as a guide as the notion of cause does: a determinist or intentional discourse functions as a possible catalyst for new practices,
which however may have nothing to do with what the discourse *says*.
Seeing our behavior as an action or as an event is always seeing it; that is,
it is something more and different than just behaving: something that
might prime a process of renewal and later might even be judged consistent with the results of that process, while it remains true that such "di-
rectionality"—however psychologically important it might be for us to
assume it—usually has little weight in the course of the process.

E: You mean that the words we use to describe our goals and intentions have no effect in moving us?

B: Some words will have effect, because words are things too, and like
all other things can interact in the world. But it won't be their *meaning*
that has effect: it will be their matter, their physical structure—what
they sound or look like. Words can spur people to action, sure, but to
know how to do that we must turn to rhetoric . . .

E: . . . or to advertising.

B: Right! We must invoke disciplines that philosophers, not by
chance, have always opposed and ridiculed, rather than the philosophical discipline par excellence, Plato's dialectic, the doctrine of definitions
and concepts. Meaning is nothing but an abstraction, that is, ultimately,
a loss, and if words have effect it is precisely insofar as they have *not* lost
their contact with (other) things, insofar as they are able to set our perceptual structure in motion.

R: Beyond this rhetorical possibility, then, freedom, plans, and desires are just worthless tales.

B: Once more, I wouldn't put it in such drastic terms: tales have a
function, and earlier we tried to figure out what that was.

E: But when we tried to do so, you took a strangely "objective" position: you talked about how things stand, how individuals of a certain
species behave. It almost seems that Angelo combines an idealist philosophy with a realist metaphilosophy.

B: Your point is well taken, and this combination is significant in two
ways. First, it's important strategically: if for the idealists philosophy is

no longer a mirroring of reality but is rather dream, invention, transgression, one must still always speak with the realists. To avoid the risk of isolation one must try to convince them *in their own terms* of the advantages of such an activity. Second, and remaining now within the idealist perspective, stories and inventions will be such only if there are several of them, in continuous dialectical conflict with one another: through that conflict, that debate, and the consequent articulation, through their interminable chasing each other and getting more and more twisted as a result, they will *show*, with more eloquence than anything that could be *said*, their nature as stories. So it is essential that the idealist story contain a constant reference to the opposite one: paradoxically, if it routed the competition, if it triumphed in the last inconclusive verbal war and declared its total autarky, it would make scorched earth not only for the other stories but also for itself—and would become reality.

Eight

ENRICO: Let's return to our story, then, since we may have to complicate it somewhat. So far, the relation between freedom and facts, between actions and the world of happenings, has been presented as one of exclusion and contrast, or of parallelism if you will: freedom and facts might presuppose each other, but only as counterparts, as terms of comparison. Their contacts take place in a no man's land inhabited by spies and dominated by secrets; their coexistence is a tension at the limit, a Sisyphean squaring of the circle. How then do we get to the point of thinking (because people certainly do think that way: for example, Stefano does) that freedom is, quite simply, *part* of the facts? How can the primordial freedom of reading and interpreting the world enter *into* the world?

BERTOLDO: Grammar makes it enter there; or rather, grammar forces us to think that it has entered.

E: You must explain that.

B: We have already seen that attributing experience to the I is a fundamental component of our form of life, and we have emphasized some consequences of that attribution: the necessity of constituting a subjective/objective dichotomy, of conceiving both terms of that dichotomy as coherent positions, of translating the subject's freedom into the regularity

of a law. What we did not yet sufficiently bring into focus is the fact that
the word "I" belongs to the same language as every other word, and
hence like every other word it can be used to talk about the world.

E: Thus the "I think" becomes an empirical I.

B: Exactly. Suppose I say, "Bertoldo stands up": this sentence describes a bit of world history, an event, the behavior of some definite object, and it's entirely irrelevant that it is I who says it. Whether it's true
or false, it is that independently of the point of view from which it is uttered. But now suppose that I say, "I stand up." This sentence too talks
about the world, predicates something of an object, but through the use
of the pronoun "I" it becomes clear that that object is the same as the
subject, that the topic of this narrative is the same as the narrator, that
it's the narrator's story that is being told, the story of *his* standing up.
The logic of this pronoun brings out an identification, an identity . . .

E: . . . which takes the subject's objectivity for granted . . .

B: . . . that is, presupposes as already completed the Sisyphean task
you mentioned earlier, assumes that the realization of an impossibility
has already occurred—with devastating results. For identity entails
sharing the same properties, and that entailment gets a relentless dialectic in motion. As an *object* of discourse, the object of a narrative, the I
can be treated like any other object: what it does can be explained in
terms of other things that happened, and the latter in terms of yet others, and so on indefinitely. As an object, in short, the I will not be the
master of its own standing up, or of its own wanting to stand up, but the
I is also something else: it is also the subject, the narrator to which we
have ascribed the free choice of a vocabulary, the original assumption of
a level of reality. By the use of "I," the subject gets projected onto the
world of objects *and hence* the freedom which is a necessary component
of the concept of a subject must also be projected onto that world—a
world constitutionally foreign, opposed, inimical to it. For the subject to
be able to tell its story, for it to be legitimate to say that what is being told
is the subject's story, freedom must have a place in it.

E: Any old place, you mean?

B: That might be too weak, but certainly it may be different places in
different circumstances, depending on the empirical data we favor and
let ourselves be guided by. Psychology might suggest that we assign the
subject function to some conscious or unconscious agency, and sociol-
ogy that we find it instead in some political or educational structure; in
any case, any such situating of the subject in the universe of objects will
always be partial and open to revision, because it will run against the

spirit that controls that universe, the explanatory spirit which always refers to something else. And yet, again, the use of the pronoun "I," because it sanctions the identification between the subject and *some* object, will impose on us the task of finding a suitable object, one of which it is legitimate, at least temporarily, to predicate freedom.

ROBERTO: Another unfulfillable task, if I understand you correctly.

B: It depends, because there are at least two tasks here. There is the task of finding a free object once and for all—which is indeed unfulfillable—but also that of finding such an object each individual time, in the particular contexts where we need it, within the particular narratives where we find ourselves using the first-person singular pronoun. In some cases, to give content to freedom, it will be enough to cite the fact that no physical constraint acts on a given body, *our* body, that this body is not handcuffed or gagged or double-locked away. But then we will note that culture, society, and education tie us up much more effectively than any rope, and will search for freedom in our disposition to dissent, to contestation. And sometimes this won't be enough either: we will feel "involved in the same dirty game" even as we criticize it, and will revolt against the slimy "tolerance" that swallows and assimilates everything, and will want to abstract ourselves totally in some kind of devilish violence or complete ataraxy.

E: It was not by chance that you spoke of dialectic before: for it seems that we have slowly moved from the second antinomy to the third one.

B: Yes, though notice that this dialectic has not only a metaphysical meaning, like the Kantian one, but also an emotional aspect. The project of constituting an I, as we described it, is a destructuring one, a project of revolt, of opposition to everything that is in the name of what is not (and possibly *ought to* be). As an I, the I is not, can't be, an object like all others, indeed it can't be an object at all: objectifying it is straining it, however necessary that might be to give concreteness to its criticisms, weight to its objections. So the I, or better the tension toward an I, the search for an I, insofar as it calls in question and possibly eats away at the consolidated confidence of tradition and practice, is also a natural source of uncertainty, of vertigo, of terror. Initiating this search means facing a risk, so it's not surprising if many prefer the beaten path of alienation; that is, if they give up looking for a cipher that identifies them, that makes them be *one*, at war with all other, undifferentiated members of a community or a world.

E: The world to which vertigo and terror are functional . . .

B: . . . and physical pain too, as you brilliantly inferred.

E: On the other hand, one may also succumb to the risk you're talking about. The search for an I may lead to madness.

B: In the process of cultural mutation that made possible the institution of an I, the madman is a monstrosity: a being who could not resist the tension, who, once the ancient rituals were challenged and destroyed, was not able to survive their loss . . .

E: . . . and ended up replacing them with other rituals, more idiosyncratic and less adaptive.

B: Well said. What we see of madness is mostly a set of defense mechanisms against it, against the void and the anxiety that *are* madness. We see the obsessive ceremonies, the phobias, the hysterical symptoms, but all that is already part of a solution of the problem, unsatisfactory as it may be. Angelo would say that there is a profound resemblance with philosophy here.

E: A rather predictable thesis: considering the relations that exist between philosophy and subjectivity on the one hand, and subjectivity and madness on the other, it is reasonable to expect that philosophy and madness will go hand in hand.

B: In fact, in the case of philosophy too what we see—and what goes under the name of philosophy—is often only a form of protection *from* philosophy: from the transgression, the play, the perverse pleasure of wandering.

E: Are you talking about philosophers' intellectual terrorism?

B: Yes, I am talking about the jargon, the learned quotes, the snobbishness: all profoundly reassuring things, hence also intrinsically *anti*philosophical ones.

R: I don't understand how terrorism can be reassuring.

B: In the same way the police can be: by frightening subversives and protecting the established interests.

E: But there is a stylistic tension in what you say, which already struck me when you talked about alienation. On the one hand you associate alienation and terrorism with confidence and stability, hence ultimately with desirable things; on the other, words like "alienation" and "terrorism" are clearly burdened with negative value judgments, and your tone suggests that you agree with those judgments.

B: You're right: the prevailing ideology, which colors my formulations too, is all on the I's side, on the side of freedom, of inquiry, often to the point of forcing the issue and suggesting misleading descriptions of the facts. This point came up before, when we were discussing explanation, which should get us closer to the *explanandum* and instead takes us further away from it; here the situation is analogous. The I is conceived as a center of force, as an oasis of peace which, once reached, will resolve all our tension and uneasiness, and resting content with an "alienating" life (the very choice of the term is highly suggestive) is seen as a source of destabilization and crisis. Whereas that source is precisely the I, the project of an I: to quiet down one must precisely *forget* the I and let practices take over, submit to constant, unchallenged habits, to what is done without asking why. It's precisely from the I that issues the search for the other, for something different; the I is the foundation of that dissatisfaction which invites us to deny what exists, and to travel along ever more deviant, ever more tortuous paths.

E: There remains the mystery of this disparity between real facts and ideological values.

B: The solution of the mystery may be that we need both habits and transgression, and if the former already have all the facts on their side, the latter has only the values left.

E: Which would allow us to explain grammar's mystifying role too: in particular, its presenting the unfeasible objectification of the subject as already happily completed.

B: Sure: this is how the ideology expressed in language can have it both ways—promote inquiry while also taming it, denying its revolutionary character. The I already exists: it's only a matter of finding it (again), of resolving the inconvenient but inessential complication of its temporary hiding.

STEFANO: Very interesting, but in all of this we have slowly gotten lost. Earlier I complained because your "freedom" had none of that moral dimension, that connection with responsibility and guilt, which is usually attributed to it, which indeed has often been used to prove its existence: if it makes sense to utter moral judgments, and if a moral judgment is meaningless in the absence of an actual capacity to choose one's behavior, then such a capacity must be acknowledged, perhaps not always but at least for those moral judgments we regard as legitimate . . .

R: Alternatively, one could recognize that morality, too, is an illusion, just like freedom.

S: Don't interrupt me, Roberto, or I'll get even more confused. So I complained about this lack of consideration of an essential coordinate of the discourse on freedom: the relation between freedom and ethics. And since the object of ethics is our conduct, our actions, not (say) our automatic, involuntary movements, I brought in the concept of an action. At which point you quickly connected an action with its goal, an action's goal with the future, the future with nonbeing, nonbeing with stories, stories with reading, and gave me back that very identification between freedom and hermeneutics from which my perplexities had started in the first place. In the face of this surprise attack, and before our conversation goes "drifting" any further, I take the liberty of expressing once more my vigorous disapproval, and of asking quite plainly: what do you, or Angelo, or the Angelo you are painstakingly reconstructing or reinventing here, take to be the relation between freedom and—not action, notice, but—*moral* action?

B: Good question, Stefano, which I too asked Angelo; but I did not understand his answer, because I caught him in one of his most lowbrow clownish moments and he just told me an odd story.

E: Really? What story?

B: He said: "Look, it's like a pyramid scheme. You send a dollar to ten people, and each of them sends a dollar to ten more people, and so on, and after a certain number of steps everyone should have a thousand dollars, you and the ten people you sent a dollar to and the thousand people who sent a dollar to you. Everyone *should*, we say, but it doesn't work that way at all: you might be able to cash in, and if you do, so will those who came before you, but after a while no one will see a penny anymore."

S: And this is all he said?

B: That's right. Then he went on to something else.

S: But that's deeply irritating! Who does he think he is, to give cryptic answers like that?

E: A genius, and most likely he's not one. But on these themes he often has interesting things to say, and hence it's worth giving him a little rope—considering also that he's not here and so cannot use it as a further incentive for his pride. So, let's see: what is the problem with pyramid schemes?

R: That to work they would need an infinite domain, but because humankind . . .

B: There, I believe that's the decisive element: in other circumstances I've heard him associate the finitude of our experience with guilt, hence with moral responsibility.

S: OK, but associate *how*? You mean guilt as a limitation, evil as lack of good?

E: No, not so directly. We must try to concentrate on what is for him the original situation of freedom, that is, reading, and from there get to responsibility and guilt.

B: Yes, and there must also be something more specific in this story of the pyramid scheme; it can't just be the dilemma finite/infinite, or he would have used some other example—perhaps a segment and a straight line.

R: What seems most specific in this case is that it's a potentially infinite repetition of the same gesture, which however ends up clashing with the limitations of the sphere in which the gesture is performed.

S: OK, but what would be the repeated gesture in the case of freedom?

E: Gentlemen, I believe I understand!

S: Very good, so enlighten us.

E: Let's begin with the freedom of synthesizing the world. At a certain moment, in a certain context, the subject will constitute, for example, a blackboard, but in other contexts, at other moments, it might constitute instead a set of elementary particles, or perhaps some mereological object blackboard+chalk+eraser. And the same thing holds for the subject insofar as it constitutes itself as an object: the I could synthesize itself as a human body, or as a particular organ or function of such a body, or also as an Id, or a Super-Ego, or a people, or a state. It *could*, notice, could *theoretically*; in practice, it's not always able to.

S: What do you mean?

E: Suppose you're God. Your time is infinite. Your powers are, too, but we are not interested in that now: time is enough. In fact, to be more precise, it's enough that you think of your experience, that you conceptualize it, as infinite. With this mental framework you put yourself before the content of spacetime . . .

B: Angelo would say, à la Kant, "before the spatiotemporal manifold."

E: OK. So you put yourself before this manifold, and you synthesize a blackboard. Your synthesis must be conceived as an action: the manifold as such does not determine this construction more than any other. There is an element of arbitrariness, an unexplained element, in your ontological choice; otherwise it would not be a choice. It's also true, however, that tomorrow you could act differently, that you have as much time as you need to make other choices, and probably, since you have that time, you will make them.

S: It's a very peculiar God you're talking about, always busy synthesizing the world.

E: And what's the use of God, if not as a guarantee that things are, and continue to be when we are not aware of them? But if you prefer, put it Descartes's way and call this fictional being a genius, possibly an evil

one. It's not the fiction as such that I'm interested in, but the new light
it throws on *our* experience, that is, on an experience whose very subject
conceives of it as finite.

S: Why finite? I don't understand that. It's a commonplace to say that
we are not able to conceive of our mortality, to think of a world that does
not contain us anymore (or does not contain us yet).

E: You're right: there is certainly a tension here. We know that we are
finite, but we never quite assimilate this knowledge emotionally, nor do
we ever master it intellectually. I confess, however, that the meaning of
this tension now eludes me, so allow me to reduce it to one of its elements and finish up what I was going to say.

S: Go ahead, though I don't know what value a discourse on such a
"reduced" basis can have.

E: We'll see. In a finite experience, then, a choice may be irrevocable,
a decision may become a condemnation without possibility of appeal.
You synthesize a blackboard, or synthesize *yourself* as a brain, and that
might well be your last moment of consciousness, you might not have
the time for another move. You could have made a different choice from
the one you did make, nothing forced you to make it, if something had
forced you it would not have been a choice; but now you must live—or
rather, die—with it. There will be no more choices to balance out what
happened, to reestablish an equilibrium within a long race to infinity:
you are at the end, are what you chose, and will never be anything else.

B: I begin to see the analogy with the pyramid scheme. There too one
eventually gets to the end of the line.

E: Exactly, and there too it's precisely at that point that moral considerations come in: it's because *there is* that point that everything must be
judged a fraud. If one could go on forever . . .

B: . . . no one would be at fault. Whereas the capitalistic dream of
expanding without paying a price is destined to become a nightmare.

R: Wait a minute, before going on let's make sure that we are all on the
same wavelength. I, for one, did not understand the necessity of making
moral judgments. OK, choices made within a finite experience may be
irrevocable, but why should they also be good or evil?

B: I may be able to answer that question. Enrico pointed out that in a
limited domain a distribution problem inevitably becomes a political
one, that is, it connects with the administration of a certain *power*.
That's why I mentioned capitalism earlier: in that case too, since resources are finite and the consumers' needs and desires are potentially
infinite, it will be a matter of imposing on consumers a certain logic for

the assignment of resources, and the idea that such a political move can be avoided through an interminable and indiscriminate expansion will only have the purpose of concealing ideologically what move was actually made.

R: OK, but in the case of freedom, or if you will the freedom to read, what are the resources? And who are the consumers?

B: However strange it might sound to you, the consumers—or better the potential consumers—are all possible readings of certain data. And the fundamental resource to which this "population" aspires is existence, being in the world.

R: Now you're falling into mysticism! What do you propose, an unexhausted desire of incarnation on the part of wandering souls?

E: Not precisely, because we are not taking the souls' point of view. It's rather from the point of view of whoever realizes their incarnation—less metaphorically, whoever synthesizes certain objects and is forced to interpret this operation as a choice—it's for him that the problem arises of justifying what he does, of legitimizing the particular distribution that was realized through him, of overcoming the casualness, the arbitrariness of this state of affairs.

S: You mean overcoming the freedom of the choice?

E: That too, since the finite nature of experience has made him face the *negative* consequences of that choice, its repressive, tyrannical aspect.

S: I don't understand . . .

B: You might understand better if you recalled an additional complication, which so far we have left aside. The narrator surfaced originally as a critical stance, a perspective from which to challenge all reality. Forced to objectify itself in order to give weight and substance to its criticisms, it has now come to the point of conceiving the world as its own construct, but just as it realizes this titanic ambition, its finite nature puts it in a blind alley: *its* world has crystallized by now, *exists*, and there is less room left—maybe none at all—to continue the endless task of denying all that is. Time may be up.

E: That's right, the I's finitude sets it in contradiction with itself, with its mission, and the need for justification is just a pathetic attempt to avoid the contradiction.

R: But how is this justification possible?

E: I don't know that, and I don't believe Bertoldo and Angelo know either; perhaps it's another unfulfillable task. But that's not our problem: we wanted to know why there *had to* be a justification, not whether there *could* be. If there can't be, then perhaps our construction of the world will always be lived as a crime, a pure act of domination, a groundless *hybris*, an unmotivated repression of latent, unexpressed potentialities. And that may very well be how we do live this construction, it may be the original sin; but it's a sin we tirelessly try to escape, undauntedly attempt to deny. We deny it by explaining how the choices made *had to* be made, though not in a causal sense, of course, because a choice is free, not necessitated by previous events. But to refuse that kind of necessitation—which is to say, ultimately, of rationalization, of comprehension, of explanation—means only to pose the question of what other necessitation can be offered, in what other terms. Saying that a choice was *good*, or that it was *imperative* for us to make it, is nothing but a coded formulation of this problem: then we'll have to crack the code, interpret the message, articulate our need, which we will do in many different ways, perhaps always leaving, irreparably, a residue of dissatisfaction, a pointed finger that continues to exclude us from the paradise where tensions are ironed out, problems are solved, and questions are answered.

S: So, to recapitulate, the relation between freedom and morality . . .

B: We must distinguish, Stefano, between a specific moral theory, which understands this relation in a specific way, and the authority with which the relation imposes itself on us, demanding among other things the elaboration of such theories. It's at the second level that our discourse is located: we are talking not so much about the relation per se as about how and why we feel a need for it. We are talking about how certain words (freedom, choice) will set other words in motion (responsibility, approval, condemnation), about how sentences containing the former will necessarily find themselves, one way or another, close to sentences containing the latter. We are talking about a constellation of concepts that refer to each other, that manifest mutual resonances, without specifying in what ways the resonances occur or should occur. In such abstract and general terms, our proposal is that choosing a world within a finite experience means, or at least may mean, *definitively* choosing a world, eliminating once and for all every alternative world, everything else the world, and with it the subject, could have been. Such a potentially irrevocable decision, precisely insofar as it's lived as a decision, as a free act, an act that cannot be attributed to anyone else, throws open a perennial concern, a need to have been right, a regret for the rational order of things.

Nine

STEFANO: You seem to be saying that, in this case at least, speaking of "guilt" is the same as speaking of "lack of justification," that guilt is some sort of original state, to be resolved through theorizing, that in short there's nothing specifically *evil* one must do in order to be guilty.

BERTOLDO: If you think about it, it's not so strange. What are our evil actions after all, what does the typically human evil reduce to? To denying, repressing, violating our fellow human beings and asserting ourselves: violating them in their abilities to act, to express, and to enjoy themselves so as to promote instead *our* bodies, our activity, and our enjoyment. But where will be the limits of this violation, how shall we distinguish the simple, "natural" impulse of self-preservation and pursuit of one's own well-being from abuse, from greed, from scorn? By providing reasons, justifications: by conceiving others not as things, as means, as commodities, but rather as ends, as intelligences equal to ourselves with whom we must reach an agreement, to whom we must give an account and explain what authorizes our egoism.

ENRICO: There surfaces again the relation between society and guilt.

B: Yes, and with it the Freudian themes Roberto liquidated a bit simplistically as myths. Acknowledging others means admitting limits to one's omnipotence, to one's desire. It means judging that desire a possible mistake, raising the problem of redeeming oneself from that mistake; without this act of self-accusation "the others" would disappear, would reduce to pure bodies, would not constitute a community. We have not yet arrived at *these* others, the ones who really exist, the actual members of the human tribe, but is it surprising if even with respect to those purely potential others who are the other myselves, even in the case of that self-affirmation and self-preservation which are situated within the choice of an I, "unjust" reduces in practice to "unjustified," "lacking a justification," and good coincides with a *non*doing: that is, not doing what we cannot give a reason for?

ROBERTO: A reason we would not need, on the other hand, if we denied the intervention of freedom in the constitution of the world.

B: But whoever is not satisfied with that evasion will find himself forced to accept a sense in which something *must* be and yet *might not* be, something is legitimate and rational and *owed* and at the same time not inevitable: the sense in which we speak of moral obligation.

E: In fact, the distinctive characteristic of deontic modalities is that the principle of necessity does not hold for them.

S: In conclusion, we would be not only free to read but also guilty for it?

B: Why not? Wasn't it from the tree of knowledge that we were forbidden to eat?

S: Yes, but that was the knowledge of good and evil!

B: That is, a knowledge which would let us substitute some content for the enigmas represented by those words, and finally understand why what we chose to do had to be done, why the world where we chose to live was the one we had to live in. Don't forget that Adam before he sinned—or perhaps I should say: before becoming aware of his sin—occupied his time assigning names to the other creatures, that is, synthesizing them.

E: All this is highly suggestive, Bertoldo, but the example of the Garden of Eden may be misleading, in that it excludes an aspect we should rather focus on.

B: What do you mean?

E: Adam and Eve are alone in the presence of God, who constitutes their entire public; our moral judgments instead (as you yourself recalled) contain a more or less explicit reference to a community of individuals, all equal before the law. Kant has even regarded the notion of morality as equivalent to that of generalizability, of universalizability of one's behavior, or rather of the maxims that guide and regulate that behavior; considering how close Angelo is to Kant, I would expect that at some point his subject, his free, responsible, and moral "I," makes room for a "we," for a kingdom of ends in which might be realized that agreement, that integration among different wills you mentioned earlier.

B: You're right, Enrico: we must indeed arrive at the others, at our fellow humans, if we want to give a plausible account of moral experience. But unfortunately on this theme Angelo has never expressed himself clearly: he prefers to slip from "I" to "we" and vice versa, depending on the circumstances . . .

E: . . . as Kant does.

B: Yes, though I believe that both have enough conceptual tools to address the problem. Perhaps we could do it for them, despite the risks of misunderstanding such an operation involves.

E: After all, even if we did not reconstruct their position exactly, what we reconstruct might have some independent interest.

B: OK, let's try then. As I see it, we should begin with this remark: since objects and concepts belong to distinct categories, an object must never be reducible to a concept, a predicate. There must always be something more in an object than in any concept under which it falls; no concept must be able to exhaust it . . .

E: So Leibniz was wrong in equating objects with individual concepts.

B: Yes. An object is not an *infima species*: even if in fact a species contains only one object, this must not be a matter of necessity. It must be at least possible for every species, however determinate, to include a multiplicity of individuals. *Every* species, you understand: every description, every characterization, every "nature," and every "essence."

E: So freedom too . . .

B: I see you got it right away, but let's go one step at a time. When freedom first entered our discourse, it was still the subject's freedom, the freedom of the narrator who chooses a vocabulary in which to tell the world. Then, however, we posed the problem of telling this narrator's story, of turning the narrator from a subject into an object of discourse, of giving it a body, a location in space and time, and we got involved in a first dialectic: an object can be identical with the subject only if it's free, but objects are constitutionally necessitated, etc., etc. The theme surfacing now suggests that there is an additional dialectical conflict in this area of our reflections, an additional source for those unsatisfiable demands that worried Roberto so much. For we cannot limit ourselves to speaking of *one* free object, of *one* object which is also a subject: if there is one, it must be possible that there be more.

E: That is, that there be a community, and thus we have moved from the "I" to the "we," we have arrived at the "fellow humans" we were missing.

B: Yes, and with respect to such fellow humans the subject's freedom will go through an additional development. Born as arbitrary choice, articulated later as consistency of intentions and plans, and then again burdened with the responsibility of its own finitude, it now comes to be qualified by a set of specific limitations, which transform it from a unique, undifferentiated freedom into a set of distinct freedoms: the civil liberties. Which, come to think of it, are nothing but *residues* of freedom: freedom of speech, for example, is the maximum of freedom compatible with the existence of other thinking subjects, endowed with equal dignity and freedom. It's all the freedom one can have without abusing others.

E: Certainly an absolute monarch has greater freedom.

B: And that's why he's called "absolute": disconnected, that is, *absolutus*, from every tie and every constraint, from every limitation. The freedom of the members of a community, on the other hand, is always relative, regulated . . .

E: . . . which sometimes has paradoxical results, as when everyone is allowed to have his own absolute values.

B: Are you referring to freedom of religion?

E: Yes: what you say emphasizes the "critical" nature of this case. A religious faith is, I'd say by definition, totalizing, global, fundamental; it constitutes the basis of every other belief, of every possible argument, the basis that must not be called in question . . .

B: I understand. Therefore just admitting the possibility of *multiple* faiths means weakening them all . . .

E: . . . or fragmenting the community: reducing it to a multiplicity of groups with only internal (mutual) recognition . . .

B: Returning now to our more general theme, the expansion of freedom in the modern world has meant an expansion of the *number* of free subjects, of the scope of the free community, which in turn was only possible if the *quantity* of freedom available to each subject was reduced. In fact, it was not so much an expansion of freedom as of justice, of *Recht*.

E: What do you mean?

B: I was already talking about this earlier by analogy, apropos of the metaphorical community of the many myselves; now we can face the issue more explicitly. Justice amounts to justification, and the so-called expansion of freedom has meant primarily an expansion of the number of people before whom one must justify oneself, who have the right to demand a justification—hence the necessity of finding *more* justifications for one's behavior, of attributing a higher degree of justice to oneself.

S: But your equating justice and justification seems dangerous to me. Everyone has his reasons for doing what he does: even in this trial the defendant has brought forth all sorts of excuses.

B: More than that: He's not brought them forth personally, accepting the risks that his lack of competence would have entailed. The law required (as it always does) that he be assisted by a dedicated professional, aware of all the rules and all the tricks of the trade, and that it be the latter who presented his reasons as convincingly as possible. Even someone accused of the most horrible crime is a subject, who must be granted the same rights as anyone else.

S: OK, but let's not overdo it: in this case it is just to recognize that the justifications are fallacious and wrong, it is just to reject them.

B: I don't deny that, but why? Why do we first assign ourselves the duty (and assign the accused the right) to hear him out, indeed to listen to an almost "ideal" formulation of his perspective, and then consider ourselves authorized to convict him? Because any of us could be in his place, because his perspective could be ours, and it's for the sake of each of us, even more than for his sake, that we search for a reason—a reason which, precisely because of that, cannot be an idiosyncratic one but must rather make an identification possible, present itself as potentially accessible to all . . .

E: Self-defense, for example.

B: That's right. If the defendant showed that he killed in self-defense, everyone could share that motivation and one could not accuse him of having exceeded the limits imposed on our freedom by civil society: he would have behaved like anyone else in his place, that is, like any of those other agents to whom similar rights must be assigned.

S: Your position doesn't hold water, Bertoldo. If we were all moved by the same egoism, that is, by the same supreme contempt for everyone else's interest (and pain), egoism would be an extremely general motivation—indeed the most general possible. But I don't believe we would consider it a justification.

B: You're right, Stefano: I spoke with more haste than lucidity. I shouldn't have said, "he would have behaved like anyone else in his place," but rather, "he would have behaved in a way that anyone else (in a society of equals) would approve of."

S: And what's the difference?

B: A profound one. To begin with, clearly the object of our judgments is not the behavior per se but the intention it reveals—Kant would say (as Enrico recalled earlier), the "maxim" that guides it. So this is what I refer to when (for the sake of brevity) I speak of the *way* someone behaved.

S: So far, I have no objections: I too spoke about motivations.

R: *I* have an objection. Didn't we say that intentions are a ghost in the machine, an attempt to hide the fact that we can't explain something?

B: Yes, but we also said that it's entirely legitimate to use the word "intention" as the variable "x" is used in algebra: to remind us of the presence of an unknown value. To solve the equation containing that variable we will have to study a person's whole behavior, look for its logic; when it seems that we have found it, we will advance a conjecture as to what intention moved him . . .

E: Which means, if I understand you correctly: we will advance hypotheses as to what his next moves will be.

B: Exactly: to say that a person behaved in a certain way out of egoism, or to save his life, means to make a commitment about what the person will do next. That being clear, suppose now that in a given situation a kills b out of egoism; it's entirely possible, as Stefano suggested, that anyone else, call him c, if put in a's place, would behave like him. In all these cases the agent's motivation would be the same (*self-love*); so, according to the formulation I gave earlier, this would be a just motivation. But of course it isn't. To see that, we must move to the new formulation, which requires us to consider not so much what c would do in a's place as rather the judgment he would give if he were *not* in a's place. Could c, if he were not in a's place, approve of a's behavior? The answer is clearly negative: if a acted on the basis of the motivation *self-love* (which for him means *love for a*), for c this motivation becomes *love for c*, and even if c (as is probably the case) feels the whole force of *this* love, that would not constitute a reason for a's behavior (if indeed c is not in a's place). In the case of self-defense, however, the motivation could be *to save an innocent member of society*, and c would probably share this motivation even if it were not directly relevant to him, considering that in different circumstances it could become relevant.

E: So your proposal is based on the Kantian notion of a rational and impartial spectator . . .

B: . . . as additional evidence of its humanistic character. Once the fundamental moral notion of approval was reserved to God: it was He who was pleased with His work, and later praised and blamed the deeds of His creatures—from whom, however, He remained distant and foreign, by whom He was unnamable, inconceivable. Whereas now it's each one of us who approves (or disapproves), precisely as a representative of *all of us*.

E: Well said, and the reference to Kant suggests an additional remark. It might be possible to conceive the expansion of justice and *Recht* as an expansion of freedom too, in contrast with your earlier statement.

B: You must be thinking of a freedom different from pure and simple absence of constraints.

E: Yes, and that's where Kant comes in, since he calls the absence of constraints negative freedom, and then raises the problem of finding a positive variant of it. He finds that variant to be autonomy, which we have already discussed, but perhaps what he says can be extended and deepened in the light of the relation between subject and community. Suppose that you are under no constraints: you can do anything, anything you want, but what does that "can" mean? Only that no one forces you to do anything, not that you really have the *capacity* to act in some way, a way which is actually at your disposal. If you have that capacity, it may be possible to identify the law of your behavior (which is what worries Kant), but the question I intend to consider now is: how does one acquire that capacity? How does one acquire *any* capacity?

B: With practice.

E: Sure, but before practice comes what makes it possible, that is, example: we see someone else move that way and slowly, gradually, we learn to imitate him. Thus in the end freedom as a real possibility, as the real availability of some behavioral strategies, requires confronting paradigmatic instances of them. The absence of constraints offers us an empty stage on which theoretically anyone could play, but in order to fill that stage it's necessary that someone start playing, and the more actors do so the more roles will be within our reach.

B: I see now in what sense you spoke not just of deepening but extending what Kant says: in a community, positive freedom gets substantiated for each of us in a multiplicity of possible "laws."

E: That's right: by conceiving myself as a member of a community of equals, I will regard every other member as another potential myself, and will be able to use *his* habits, *his* practices, to broaden the spectrum of operational modes among which to choose . . .

B: . . . and also, returning to the original significance of the constitution of a free I, to disrupt the habits already consolidated, to overcome the inertial resistances of the existing structure.

E: So positive freedom, freedom as really *being able* to do something, not only is not in contrast with the regulation imposed by communal life, but in some sense even presupposes it—a bit like what we said earlier about freedom and necessity.

B: And justice, by acknowledging the impossibility of a generalized identification with the defendant's behavior, fulfills the delicate task of defending everyone's freedom, that is, of maintaining that potential equality which is a premise for interchangeability, and hence for possibly learning from one another, for possibly using others to enrich oneself.

E: In yet other words: for communication, for *putting in common* a repertory of moves, for the capacity to transfer the notion of equality from the abstract, conceptual level of a pure (and empty) legal demand to the empirical and concrete level of real functionality.

R: Alternatively, one could avoid so many acrobatics by declaring this man insane.

S: And letting him out on the street!

B: Easy, don't get excited. To declare him insane would mean to exclude him from the community of free agents, and hence make the concepts of justification and guilt inapplicable to him. And certainly sometimes we do that; but wanting to do it always would be one more attempt at evading a problem, at avoiding a dialectical situation by taking shelter in a form of life that does not belong to us.

E: Why dialectical? You used that expression earlier, when you introduced the need for otherness and community, but I don't understand it: I don't see where the unresolvable conflict is.

B: Think about it: the subject of this experience, of *all* this experience I decided to call mine, has nothing but this experience. By definition, no other experience could be part of it, or it wouldn't be *another* one. But the subject, in the course of its attempt at objectifying itself, at telling its own story, comes upon the conceptual need to admit other similar objects, other objects which are also subjects, subjects of other experiences. Like every such need, this one too imposes on the subject the task of a concretization, an actualization, a spatiotemporal realization, but for that realization the subject can only refer to its own experience: there is no larger scope or horizon within which to conduct the search. So how will the subject be able to find in its own experience any empirical content for what is by definition beyond that experience? Where will it locate, in what is irremediably, inextricably its own, that *other* it needs in order to speak of itself in objective terms?

E: You already suggested an answer when you spoke of one's fellow humans. One will have to look for creatures of the same species, creatures *like* oneself.

B: Unfortunately it's not that easy. Suppose that the subject has identified itself with a human body, that is, an object provided with a head, a trunk, two legs, a heart, a nervous system, and so on. So the subject has ascribed its experience to that body and, as we saw earlier, has tried to explain the features of its experience by referring to features of that body. Now surfaces the need to recognize the possibility of other objects subjects, objects carriers-of-experience, and the subject observes that within its visual and tactile field other bodies present themselves which are analogous to the one it has decided to consider its own—indeed, the one it has decided to consider *itself*. That is, there are other self-moving objects, with a head, a trunk, etc. So the subject finds it natural to satisfy its need for otherness by declaring those bodies, too, identical with subjects of experiences, with narrators, with free agents—by projecting onto them a capacity for choice like the one it was forced to admit for itself and for the body *it* is identical with. But this is nothing more than a shot in the dark, whose outcome is destined to remain forever mysterious. In its own case, the subject has both terms of the question available: it sees its body as a spatiotemporal, external object, just like any other, but it also lives its experience, feels it from the inside, and can constantly compare it with the vicissitudes of that body. However fallible the subject's hypotheses of correspondence may be, however new movements of that body may disconcert it and force it to go back to the drawing board, it remains true that in this case both series of data are available. But only in this case: in all others the subject does indeed see the bodies move, and can carefully study their structures, but nothing will ever show him that the essential element is not missing, that despite the similarities, the analogies, the resonances, no soul animates those other bodies, no representative and projective capacity expresses itself in those movements.

S: But the bodies themselves will tell him! They are talking bodies, thank God, which will be able to describe and communicate their experience to your wretched solipsist!

B: It wouldn't be enough, Stefano. Language too is a form of behavior, a datum, something external for which many explanations are possible. And as for the solipsism you accuse me of, it might not be as wretched as you think. An empirical solipsism would be wretched: a theory according to which there is only one subject in the world. But the position I'm trying to reconstruct is the exact opposite of such a theory: according to it, it's not even conceivable that there be only one subject in the world. For there to be one, it must be possible for there to be more than one. If this is solipsism, it's a transcendental variety: since the conceptual starting point is experience, since experience is objective only insofar as it is connected, structured, unitary, and since we decided to attribute this unitary experience to a subject, the rational reconstruction of the world—and hence also of the other subjects which are to be located in that world—must be carried out starting from this subject's experience.

E: As evidence for what you're saying, Bertoldo, I would cite all the difficulties that there have always been in determining the extension of humankind, that is, of the community with which the subject identifies, the set of individuals onto which it is ready to project an experience like its own. Think of the medieval debates on the incomplete and defective nature of the female soul; think of when similar questions were raised about the "savages" discovered in the new world.

R: But those were cheap ideological tricks, third-rate attempts to defend a particular hierarchy of power and exploitation! Philosophy at its worst, enslaved to a political design!

E: I have no doubts about that, Roberto, and I agree with your negative judgment, which incidentally proves you a less amoral individual than you yourself would claim . . .

R: I never said I was amoral, as an empirical individual!

E: OK. It is still true, however, that this questionable strategy was in fact used to defend a political design, and if it was used it's because it had a good chance to succeed; and that was because it was based on a natural perplexity, a genuine source of doubt, an authentic uncertainty. At any rate, if you find these examples unacceptable, consider a more fashionable problem. Take a computer and leave aside its current operational limitations and its future potentialities, about which earlier we formulated some hypotheses . . .

R: . . . fanciful ones.

E: As you wish. But now those hypotheses are irrelevant. Take something the computer can do *right now*; suppose for example that, if you press the wrong key, it tells you: "Watch out! You are ruining everything." Question: when it behaves like that, like one of us, can we say that it has the same sensations as we do, the same "internal life"?

B: The inverse of the previous problem.

E: Exactly. With women and savages, it's the structural resemblance that suggests an identity of operation; here it's the other way around . . .

B: . . . and not surprisingly there have been those who said: forget functional issues, computers don't think (hence are not subjects) because they don't have a head and a trunk and two legs. The perceptible similarity is at least as important as the operational one for deciding what is and what is not (identical with) a subject.

E: And at this point I would be tempted to launch a daring hypothesis.

B: Go ahead, we are among friends.

Ten

ENRICO: Think of the development of the Gothic novel in the early eighteen hundreds, of authors like Mary Shelley and her *Frankenstein*, and consider that that was the first generation of which we could say that it had digested Kant. It seems to me that in those works a problem surfaces that is left open by critical philosophy: the problem of the other, of what appears, what *must* appear, at the limit of our experience, pointing confusedly at the inexorable mystery of a different subjectivity, announcing the necessary and yet radically uncertain truth that there are alternatives to this whole experience, stories which are as coherent and complete as *this* story is, points of view which are as all-inclusive as ours. How can we possibly know that we have found another such point of view? For example, how do we know that that body over there, in the corner, is a subject of experience, a free agent? It looks a lot like this body, like the subject of this experience, the agent of these actions, but . . . it might have been artificially constructed, produced by the morbid imagination of a paranoid scientist, it might have cables and chips under its appearance of flesh and blood. That body speaks, initiates talk on its own and provides appropriate responses when one addresses it, but its words might be the playing out of a clever, sophisticated program, or a simple sediment left by chance. And chance, or an evil will, might explain the regularity of its movements, the inflexible logic of its behavior. Nothing of what we see will ever guarantee the presence of another subject, make us certain that we are not alone, that we are not lost in this loneliness, that we are not annihilated . . .

BERTOLDO: . . . and then from the Gothic novel comes the detective story, and what is a detective story if not an attempt to reconstruct a subjectivity, an intentionality, a project, a plan, beginning with a number of traces? And what is a trace if not an intrinsically ambiguous datum, which might mean something *other than itself* but might also turn out to be entirely opaque, to fade into everydayness, to be mortified into a well-rounded, unimpeachable objectivity, with no frills, none of those frills one needs to continue to search? Patiently, stubbornly, the detective on duty insists in interpreting the data as signs, as pieces of a still incomplete jigsaw puzzle, and meanwhile everything conspires against him, everything invites him to deny that there is a will behind those data, a person. Each of them is the outcome of a necessary concatenation of events, but a *different* one in each case: their appearing together is a pure coincidence . . .

E: . . . and one could even say that the detective story is the archetypal novel, the novel par excellence. Every novel reconstructs a subjectivity, or more than one, from a number of traces—or rather of data which it is suggested must be read as traces. Every novel is a jigsaw puzzle, where ambiguous but significant indications are skillfully dropped, so as to be gathered by the careful reader. Of that "vast fresco" every novel probably aspires to be, the pages give us only a sketchy outline: a large part of the sinopia and the color we must add ourselves, at our risk.

B: So in every novel there is at least one detective: the reader.

E: Exactly, or at least what critics call the implicit, ideal reader: the unexpressed character to whom the author sends his signals, who is able to reconstruct his plot.

B: And who might even coincide with the author himself; how often it is said that there is only one true reader for every work . . .

E: Yes, sure, but it might be the author only insofar as the latter accepts the challenge of this duplication, consents to mirror himself in someone else who listens to him, someone like him in whom to find himself.

B: And thus we return to meaning as interpretation, as conceptually situated within the public, even when there is empirical identity between the public and the author.

E: Yes, and we may understand better why the result of that check, that crisis which gets the "meaningful" confabulation started must be a shift, a differentiation, the positing of an *other* that becomes an *object* of discourse. That we ask questions about what constitutes a problem and try to comprehend it, to categorize it, is an empirical fact, which we earlier imported a bit hurriedly into our transcendental argument. But now we begin to see that that move only goes back over an original ritual, re-proposes the catharsis of the primordial problem, the search for the self: a problem that posits the original shift, that institutes the fundamental theme of which every other theme will be an echo, that establishes the very project of inquiring, of reconstructing, of making sense of that world which is the subject's most elementary and inevitable counterpart.

B: Without however being *similar* to it . . .

E: . . . and hence something similar to the subject will have to be re-sponsible for the plan, for the coherence of the world: to begin with, perhaps, the capitalized Author, the ubiquitous Person, and then, when that one comes to seem too foreign, some "incarnation" of it, and then again a community ever more historical and transient, ever closer, a community of potential and potentially interchangeable *judges* . . .

B: Judges and witnesses, which brings us back to detective stories.

E: That is, to the place where this interpretive operation shows up most openly, becomes manifest ideology, explicit task, metalanguage . . .

STEFANO: But why should death, fear, and crime enter in such an es-sential way into this archetypal novel? Why does this painstaking decod-ing of the other go through so much toil and suffering?

B: Perhaps because the other forces us to reflect on ourselves, on our own nature. If the other is like us, we too are like him, and the other dies, dissolves, turns into dust; so we will die too. If we want to come into the world, we must accept a limit to our experience, to this whole experience we attributed to ourselves.

E: So that's where the finitude comes from! And that's why, even when we accept it, we are not able to understand it, to assimilate it! It's our bet on our membership in a species—a bet we must make if we want to believe we exist as objects—that forces us to predicate of ourselves that end and that beginning which belong to all members of the species, which can be observed for all other members of it. But for us there is no such possibility of observation: we will never witness our birth and our death. Nor will we ever know whether we won the bet, whether indeed those other objects are subjects like us, and we are objects like them; thus the immediacy of our experience, of our ancient sense of being in-vincible and uninterrupted, will always have enough strength to oppose a truth which is as needed as it is unprovable.

B: I'm reminded of the most classic example of a syllogism: "All men are mortal, but Socrates is a man, therefore . . ."

E: Right! What is this example but a typical hysterical defense against a highly emotional situation? We are facing the most critical and important inference, the one over which each of us must sweat blood, which must fill each of us with anxiety; we are facing the most mysterious premises and the most agonizing conclusion, the words for the sake of which the inferential process itself exists perhaps in the first place, and our reaction is to repeat them like a rosary, repeat them until we no longer hear them, until they no longer hurt, until they are nothing but a harmless example, indeed, of something else that really matters—the logical structure, the conceptual ghosts we superimpose on life in order to hide its tragedy.

B: Whereas in detective stories that tragedy shows: since the thought of the other imposes on us the thought of death, the search for the other represented in the novel becomes a search for the one who can kill us, soaked with horror by the announced disintegration of the subject, the feared and incomprehensible end of its experience . . .

E: While it's understood that if the search fails then an equally threatening abyss opens up, and the subject risks seeing its very nature swallowed by it. Either the undifferentiated anxiety of not knowing what one is, and hence *if* one is, or the specific fear of finding out that one will not be. Either Camus or Agatha Christie.

B: Or perhaps a little of both, as in Chandler.

S: So the novel, whether or not it's a detective story, would be some sort of suicide.

E: That's more than a joke. Suicide after all might be an extreme way of establishing one's objectivity, one's existence. If I die too then I too am like these, like those who die, hence I too *am*.

B: Which explains why the person who attempts suicide often represents his death to himself, tries to have a preview of it, or at least to extend himself into "later" with letters, instructions, messages; one might almost say that he dies in order to see himself die, and thus convince himself that he belongs to the community of mortals. And it also explains why another main theme of the Gothic novel—in Poe, say—is the return from the other world: the salvation in extremis of a character who should have died but seems to have survived with the only purpose of telling us what one feels in that supreme moment.

E: When indeed it's not a ghost who returns, to tell us more knowledgeably about it. And think also of the splatter movies that are so popular with teenagers: those in which kids like them, true alter egos for the spectators, are cut to pieces, and their organs and blood are shown with cruel repetitiveness and gruesome details to audiences nailed to their chairs. What are these gloomy mass rituals, if not attempts on the part of individuals deeply disturbed in their search for an I . . .

B: . . . because of an education that provides them with few occasions for closeness, and hence identification, and hence positive freedom . . .

E: . . . and hence that makes it especially difficult for them to handle the anxiety of subjectivity, to articulate it in an accessible vocabulary, to mediate it through the construction of characters and roles. So what are these if not attempts to stage an extreme manifestation, a trial by fire of one's being in the world?

B: Or, if you will, to stage empirical realizations of the highest transcendental paradox: that in order to *be* the subject must deny itself, that is, deny its own nature as a subject, and hence ultimately cease to be itself, objectify itself to the hilt, lose its freedom, die.

S: But what would you say about the Stoic suicide: the choice of death as a supreme expression of freedom, an almost diabolical declaration that one has no need for the world? From what you say, killing oneself seems to be like crystallizing into a monument!

B: The fact is that death has two faces, Stefano, like Janus. One is turned toward the future: a future which is nonbeing, infinite distance, affirmation of irremediable otherness. By plunging into that nothingness, the person attempting suicide behaves like the ideal philosopher, that is, like one who does not limit himself to challenging reality and objectivity in words, to looking for alternatives to them in a story . . .

E: . . . while maintaining his safe and warm niche in that very reality.

B: Perhaps at a university! The suicidal choice, on the other hand, admits no compromise, accepts no half measure, is located at a level that doesn't even have a chance of contact with the world, and hence automatically takes up the most radical form of rebellion against that world.

S: And the other face?

B: It's the one turned to the past. By abandoning the world of objects, the suicidal person leaves his mark on it, a mark that from now on will be indelible, that no one will ever be able to correct. His contribution has already been made, he's finally come into the world . . .

S: Now? Not at birth?

B: No: birth was only an occasion, the beginning of a process. The subject comes into the world throughout its life, through a path that is completed only with the end of that life, when ceases the strenuous co-existence of two so different and inimical structures, the laborious translation of the subject's critical task into a repertory of practical moves and operational strategies. That labor and toil finally make room for the peace of separation: the subject deposits in the world its whole heritage, objectifies itself as much as possible, and withdraws forever into the dimension most proper to it.

ROBERTO: I'm impressed: it's quite some pulp fiction you're putting together. To be successful, though, besides death and violence there should also be a pinch of sex.

B: And why not, Roberto? Sex is but the most obvious empirical place to conduct the search for the other, to aggregate the first and fundamental community . . .

E: . . . and where it's legitimate to continue, even after adolescence (and not only in words), the irresistible, forbidden play of experimentation, of identification, of the expansion of one's individuality.

B: Without forgetting that sex presides over the other necessary and incomprehensible limit of experience, that is, its beginning, as much as violence often presides over its end.

E: And as for your sarcasm, I must repeat something I said earlier: people like pulp fiction, lots of them buy it, and this popularity demands an explanation. The very fact that such fiction is not "literary," hence not to be recommended for structural or stylistic qualities, suggests that we must look for its secret in the themes it deals with . . .

S: I realize that reading is not just a metaphor for you; but I would like us to return to our main issue.

B: OK. To summarize, the constitution of the subject as an object requires the possibility of thinking of a community of similar objects, and hence of a plurality of experiences similar to the one *this* subject has. *One* freedom, *my* freedom, cannot by itself be *freedom*: the articulation of the story that rationalizes and justifies the attribution of freedom to myself, to that object which I am, must go through the acknowledgment of the freedom of what I am not . . .

E: . . . and through the limitations that this "other than me" will impose on my being free.

B: So the need for the other will also become a need for regulation: one will have to come to terms with the other, the world will be something constituted in both an interpretive and a practical sense by a *we*, not an *I*, something on which an agreement must be reached, whose structure eludes in principle all solipsistic idiosyncrasies.

E: Thus arriving at a notion of truth that transcends the individual "perspectives"?

B: I think you're right: it must be here that truth enters Angelo's story. For here we can find two of its fundamental features: on the one hand, indeed, its capacity to oppose experience, to repudiate it, to invalidate it, to present itself as a goal that experience can at most aim at, without ever attaining it, and on the other—in a more positive vein—its connection with consensus, with agreement, its being founded on the mutual consistency of different experiences, of what appears to different subjects.

E: This agreement too, however, will be more a dialectic than a resonance: it will be what remains, ideally, when all criticisms have been raised, all objections heard, all difficulties taken into account. In the "public" universe where Angelo's discourse is situated, not only freedom but also truth is posited as a residue.

B: Yes, in fact one might say that in this universe falsity has conceptual priority over truth, as in Popper's program. Truth is not something of which one is "intimately" convinced, *in private*, it's not based on evidence and certainty, it's not realized by accumulating confirmations: it's rather what resists attacks, contrasts. And for such a truth to be, it's necessary that someone take the burden of contrasting and attacking: truth cannot originate in a soliloquy but only in a debate, in a dialogue.

E: Right: a dialogue . . .

R: But in this way you just close the circle and recover your methodological premises at a "substantive" level. You started out with Angelo's evolutionary framework, with his idea that the raison d'être for theories is not their truth, or their rationality, but rather a blind process of mutation, of casual, adventurous "drift," of continuous displacement and slippage starting from the only things of which it is legitimate to assert correctness—practices, habits, set traditions—and now what do you conclude, what world do you end up drawing? One in which what is true—hence what is, the facts, the *object* of those theories—is what survives the selection of criticism, what is left standing a minute longer than the competition, even if there is no good reason why it should be left standing.

B: What else can one do, in this profession, other than wander idly in one's logical space, trying now and then to go back to the same point, to see if in the meantime one has learned anything? And as for the evolutionary framework, you were the first to speak about the survival of individuals and groups.

R: Yes, but I spoke about it in terms that were *already* factual: since the world has a determinate structure, some moves have survival value and some don't. Whereas you use survival to *define* facts!

B: So what? If facts are part of a story, what matters after all is that one keep telling it.

S: Don't get farther afield, or I will lose my mind! I think you were summarizing, Bertoldo.

B: That's right, and I had arrived at the necessity to constitute a "we," a community. Since the subject's experience is the only experience available to it, the community will continue to elude it. The subject will be left with a hermeneutics of suspicion, with a thematization of that experience as a reservoir of indications, of traces, of signs, that is, of realities which, without ceasing to be what they are—without ceasing to be part of the same experience—intimate, express, suggest something different. As signs, those realities will necessarily be fallible: in order to be able to say that a sign has been read well, one must be able to say that it was read badly; it makes no sense to speak of correctness except in the presence of the risk of error. So the community one searches for will always only be a thesis to prove, and with it the objectivity of the subject, its nature as a free and independent object, will also always remain to be proved. Some day we will look around us and call ourselves free—all those of us who are so "fortunate"—because the door is not locked, because no one is crowding us; some other day we will find our "truest" freedom in prison, in our thoughts and projects, in the "ideal" contact with other martyrs like us; and on yet another we will feel constrained even as we dance in a wheat field, locked into that dance, those leaps and pirouettes, by who knows what nervous chemistry or social balance . . .

R: Therefore, in the last analysis, this freedom makes no difference and we could easily dispense with it.

S: In the name of what? Of an explanatory project that is at least as indeterminate?

R: Or that might define the very notion of determinacy, without being seduced by chimerical and childish pretenses.

S: Is it chimerical and childish to refuse to simplify one's life as you urge in order to avoid problems? Do you perhaps believe that my indignation at this crime is less real than your causal chain?

R: No: it's perfectly real, and like every real thing it can be explained. Because you were born in a certain place, to certain parents, you went to certain schools . . .

S: And would that be explaining? Don't you realize how much is left out of your "explanation," how much violence you're doing to my sensibility—and even to yours, if you were honest enough to admit it?

R: I don't see why an explanation shouldn't do violence. Do you think that understanding costs no effort?

S: Precisely the effort you're refusing to make!

E: It's seven-thirty, Bertoldo: the movie begins in a few minutes.

B: Let's leave quietly.